STO

ACPL IT

SO-BFQ-445

DISCARDED

# ALL ABOUT WINE

This venerable, sturdy plant is typical of the 'vines' in the vineyards of Châteauneuf-du-Pape. It is thirty years old. These vines are severely pruned each year and look like dead stumps until in early spring they come to life with vigorous new shoots. The stones, worn smooth in the glacial age, shield the soil from summer heat.

# All about Wine

*Blake Ozias*

Thomas Y. Crowell Company
New York · Established 1834

L.C. Card 67-27767

1   2   3   4   5   6   7   8   9   10

To the Memory of
Ellwood R. Burdsall
*un vrai connaisseur*

1411329

# Acknowledgments

I most gratefully acknowledge the help and guidance given me in the writing of this book by the world's two great experts, both of them my friends for over thirty years:

ANDRÉ L. SIMON, dean of wine writers, founder of the *Wine & Food Society* in 1932, still its President and the inspiration of its many affiliates in this and other English-speaking countries, author of more than fifty books on wine and food—now in his ninetieth year, hale and hearty.

FRANK SCHOONMAKER, a wine authority second to none, author of several books including his *Encyclopedia of Wine*, acknowledged to be the most complete and authoritative popular reference work on French, German, Italian and other European wines. As consultant to one of California's largest producers, he has profoundly influenced the development of the California wine industry.

I am indebted also to:

TOM MARVEL, collaborator with Schoonmaker on two important wine books (1934/41) and a life-long protagonist for high standards in the making and labelling of American wines. Now consultant to one of the principal wine companies of New York State.

H. PESTEL, Director of the important French *Institut National des Appellations d'Origine des Vins et Eaux de Vie*, who patiently provided much of the information and guidance for the important chapter on *Appellations Contrôlées*.

J. DERAMOND, Director of the French *Comité National des Vins de France*.

ALEXIS LICHINE, author of the informative and entertaining *Wines of France*, a vineyard owner in France and exporter of French wines to the U.S.

VICTOR LANSON, President of the renowned Champagne House, *Lanson Père et Fils of Reims* (France), for many of the photos reproduced in the chapter on Champagne.

# Contents

# Foreword

Art has open arms and a warm heart for amateurs; they all are given a sporting chance to challenge the professionals and teach them something. That is exactly what my friend Blake Ozias, has done. He never had, of course, the training, the experience, the opportunities, and still less the stocks of wine of a vintner, but his love of wine has long been quite as great as that of any professional wine merchant, and certainly more disinterested. He who loves takes notice, learns, understands, and remembers; and he also longs to share with others all that he knows, if and when he can. It is not given to us all to be as vocal about our loves as the operatic singers on the stage, but fortunately, Blake Ozias's love of wine is articulate; he has recorded in simple, straightforward, crystal-clear language, for the benefit of all who take an intelligent interest in a gracious way of living, hence in wine, all the knowledge which he has so enthusiastically collected, checked and stored about the more popular wines of the world.

I know it, because I have done the same but for many more years, and there is not a spark of jealousy in a wine-lover's heart; the more people there are who share his understanding and love of wine, the happier he will be.

This is why I welcome the publication of this book in which the uninitiated will learn so much that is of fascinating interest about wine. May it bring to a great many men and women, be they young or not so young, some valuable knowledge as well as a greater measure of joy and good health.

ANDRÉ L. SIMON

# Introduction

To get the most out of anything you have to know something about it. Wine has much to offer. Wine brings cheer, wine is good for your health, wine is a 'conversation piece'. It's a collectors' item, a delightful hobby, an indispensable ingredient of gracious living. In fact wine 'has everything', and this little book aims to introduce you to it.

For thousands of years wine has been the inseparable companion of civilization. Horace, the Roman poet, declared in 40 B.C.: 'A day without wine is a day without sunshine.' Louis Pasteur, the great French scientist, wrote a century ago: 'Wine is the most healthful and hygienic of beverages.' And to get right up to date, Ancel Keys, the well-known dietician, in his book *Eat Well and Stay Well*,[1] writes: 'All honest dry wines have a place at the civilized table,' and adds: 'You will find it pleasant and profitable to learn a little about wines.'

I have enjoyed writing this little book, for I have enjoyed wine for the greater part of a long life. My health is good and wine has brought me many lasting friendships. I hope the book will stimulate—especially in the younger generation—a wider appreciation of wine's many virtues. A knowledge of wines should be a part of everyone's education. To walk about with an Arts degree and be ignorant of wine is incongruous. I could put up strong arguments for including wine in the curriculum of all high schools and colleges.

[1] Doubleday & Co. Inc., New York.

11

Wine books are brought out in this country at an estimated rate of 1.2 a week but most of them, though entertaining and instructive to the seasoned wine lover, are too thick and too 'expert' for those who would like to serve and enjoy wine but know little about it. What is needed, I thought, is a *thin* book which, while giving the essential facts about wine and glimpses of its captivating centuries-old history, would serve essentially as a practical guide.

This is a thin book but you will find it packed with the kind of information you need to enjoy wine and reap the benefit it brings to the Art of Good Living. You can read it in an hour or two and then keep it handy to refresh your memory—and to settle arguments.

B. O.

# What Is Wine?

Wine is the subject; let me define it. True wine, a living product, is the fermented juice of freshly gathered and promptly crushed wine grapes, not of any other fruit. Good wine is not made from table or raisin grapes. The grapes must be ripe, or nearly so, else they will not contain enough sugar to support fermentation. If they are not promptly pressed and crushed after being gathered, the 'bloom' which contains yeast germs will be lost and fermentation will not take place properly.

There are many species of grapes from which wine can be made, but outside North America only one, the *Vitis vinifera*, is cultivated. This is the wine of ancient Greece and is today the only species cultivated in Europe—and anywhere else except in the United States.

Here the early discoverers found many native species and varieties, and some of these have been developed into the bearers of grapes from which good wine is made. However, in the better vineyards of California—by far the largest wine-growing area in America—the vine is the *Vitis vinifera*, imported from Europe.

*Where wine grapes grow*
Wine grapes thrive and mature best only in a temperate climate—in a belt around the world approximately between the 35th and 45th parallels, north and south of the equator. North of the 45th[1] wine grapes will not

[1] Europe is an exception: the northern boundary of the wine-belt reaches up as far as the 50th parallel.

13

ripen properly or, if they do, will contain too little sugar to support thorough fermentation. The 45th north is roughly a line running through southern New England, the Mohawk Valley in New York State, Lake Erie and westward to Northern California. South of the 35th parallel the summers are too hot—good for table grapes but not for wine grapes.

The most northern wine-growing area in the United States is the Finger Lakes section in New York State and the most southern is North Carolina and the Ozarks in Missouri and Arkansas. Comparatively little wine of value is grown in these southern areas. Wine grapes will not mature in England—too far north.

The most northern wine-growing area in Europe is in south-western Germany in the valleys of the Rhine and Moselle Rivers. In the southern hemisphere, wine is grown in Chile, in South Africa and in southern Australia.

The finest wines of the world are grown in France and Germany. France produces more fine wines than any other country and, one may truthfully add, more poor wines as well.[1] A fine point: Germany produces one tenth as much wine as France. Both countries produce some equally fine wines, but the *ratio* of fine wines to total output is higher in Germany than in France.

America is now producing many excellent wines in considerable quantities but none has so far achieved the supreme characteristics of the finest French and German wines. Below this high level the good table wines, for everyday drinking, from a number of American vine-

[1] In the production of ordinary wines, France and Italy are neck and neck as to volume.

yards, are superior to much of the *vin ordinaire* of France, Italy and Spain.

*Red, White and Rosé*

Wine comes in three colours—red of varying depths, white, which is not white but shades of straw colour, and rosé (ro-zay), a brownish pink. All three have about the same alcoholic content—from 10 to 13 per cent.[1] I state this fact to correct the false impression held by many, that white wine is less 'potent' than red, and that rosé, having such a lovely colour, should be about the most delicate of the three.

Red wines get their colour from the skins of the grapes during the process of fermentation. In making red wine the whole fruit is crushed and this mixture of skins, seed, pulp and stems, called 'must', goes directly to the fermentation vats. The skins provide not only colouring matter but, with the seeds and stems, tannin and trace quantities of mineral and nitrogenous elements which contribute to the taste of red wine, and to the good health that sound wine promotes.

White wines are made of either white or black grapes. The grapes are crushed in the same manner as for red wine, but if white wine is to be made from black grapes only the juice, gently squeezed from the crushed fruit, is fermented. The chief grape of Champagne is the Pinot Noir, a black grape. Generally speaking, white wines have rather a more delicate taste than the reds since none of the flavour of the skins, seeds and

[1] The white wines of the Moselle valley and some of the lighter Rhine wines may have no more than 8 per cent of alcohol, the wines of Alsace 9–9½ per cent and, on the high side, the very sweet white wines, stronger than any of the reds, run to as much as 15 per cent.

stems is present in the must. But there are none the less white wines that are quite as 'robust' as many of the reds. Conversely, there are some red wines that are as delicate as almost any white wine. Some of these will be mentioned later on.

Rosé is, so to speak, half-way between red and white. Its pinkish colour is obtained in different ways. In one the grapes are crushed and sent to the fermentation vats as if to make red wine. When fermentation starts, colour will begin to appear, and when the desired pink shade is reached the juice is drawn off from the skins, seeds and stems and transferred to other vats to complete its fermentation. The alcohol content of the wine is not lessened by this half-and-half operation.

Another method is to use both black and white grapes, often a number of different varieties, in the right proportions, all being combined in the fermentation vat. This mixture will give the colour wanted. The skins of the black grapes will release their colouring matter but, with the juice of white grapes present, the wine will not be red, as it would be if all the grapes were black—it will be rosé.

These two methods are the natural way and are to be preferred. The best rosé produced anywhere in Europe, in the opinion of most authorities, is *Tavel*, made in the lower Rhône valley in France, across the river from the famous vineyards of Châteauneuf-du-Pape. Here both methods are used but in either case the predominant grape is the Grenache (gren-nash), a red-wine variety that is widely grown in France, Spain and California. One of the least known but most delightful French rosé wines comes from the small village of Marsannay near

Dijon at the northern end of the Burgundy district.

All rosés are at their best when quite young and none will improve with age. In fact you will be safest if you reject any bottle with a stated vintage more than three or four years back. Its price may be attractive but that might be due, inversely, to its age.

# What Wine to Drink

For yourself, drink the wine you like; for your friends, try to give them the wine *they* like. If you don't know what you like, experiment; and when you find a wine you specially like, make a note of it in your Wine Record and at the next opportunity, try it again. You will find it of interest, too, to note where you drank it— at a friend's house or in a restaurant. If you bought the bottle at a wine shop, note the name of the shop, the price paid and the name of the shipper and the importer (see *The Wine Shipper*, page 29).

I have said drink the wine you like, but if you are to cultivate a taste for wine as a beverage to be drunk with your meals, I beg you to experiment only with *dry* wines. It is only these, not the sweet wines, that can be drunk with pleasure and satisfaction as a beverage in company with your food. A dry wine is one in which fermentation of the juice of the grapes has been complete (see *Fermentation*, page 118).

All red beverage wines are dry and so are most of the

white wines. If the very dry ones fail to appeal to your palate at first, start your experimenting with those not quite so dry—*Graves*, for instance. But *please* don't, under any circumstances, let yourself acquire a taste for sweet wine as your mealtime beverage.

Sweet wines, such as the Sauternes, are suitable only at the end of the meal along with sweet desserts. As such they are delightful and bring a final touch of perfection to a good dinner. I repeat—let red wines figure strongly in your experiments. Many of them are as delicate as most white wines. More than the white, they contain in minute quantities a number of free acids and mineral salts which add to their taste and are undoubtedly beneficial to health.

# How Can I Tell?

How can I tell, before I buy it, whether a wine is good or not?

You are planning a dinner in your home for a number of friends and you want to serve wine. If you have even a small cellar there is no problem—you select appropriate wines from those you have on hand and whose characteristics and quality you already know. But if you have to go out and buy them for this special occasion, how are you to choose them with assurance as to kind and quality?

If you know a competent wine merchant (unfortunately a rather rare species) you can ask his advice. But it will be far more satisfying if *you* tell *him*. One of the objects of this book is to make it unnecessary for you to ask anyone to choose your wines for you. In the course of the dinner someone may remark: 'This is a nice wine; what is it?' and if you yourself have selected the wines you will be able to talk intelligently about them, and your friends will surely be interested.

If you have a good wine merchant it will help him to help you if you give him a lead. Say to him, for example, 'I would like three bottles of red Bordeaux—something better than an "ordinaire" but not too costly; have you got a good Saint Julien or a Pomerol?' That should start him off on the right track and an interesting and useful conversation will ensue—and both of you will learn something new. If you don't have a good wine merchant and have to go to the average liquor store, it is unlikely that the person behind the counter will know much about the wines on the shelves. If you go to a supermarket, you will be quite on your own.

What, then, are your guide lines? The words on the bottle label will give you most of the information you need—*if you know what the words mean*. They tell you the name of the wine (the place where it came from, that is) and perhaps the name of the grower. If you are familiar with the place name you will know the general character of the wine. In the next chapter, 'Nomenclature of Wine', you will learn how wines get their names and what the names mean. With practice, which is agreeable since it involves *drinking* the wine, you will get to know dozens of wine names and the labels will mean something to you. An interesting hobby which costs nothing at all is to collect bottle labels. Soak them off the bottle and stick them up on the kitchen wall.

If the wine is French, bottled in France (as are most French wines shipped to this country), a most important guide is in the words 'Appellation Contrôlée' (see page 122). If these words are on the label you can be sure that the wine in the bottle is honest and honestly labelled. If they are not, the wine should be regarded with suspicion. Other good indicators of the quality and value of all imported wines are the names of the shipper abroad and the American importer (see *The Wine Shipper*, p. 29).

Perhaps you will want a white wine instead of a red one—or you may wish to serve both. If you want a French white wine, all that has been said above about the reds applies in the same manner to the whites. But you may like to have a German white wine. Ask your

A château-bottled wine from the commune of St. Georges-St. Emilion. 'Appellation Contrôlée': Petrus Desbois, owner of the property.

wine merchant what he has in the way of Moselle or Rhine wines—'Have you got a medium-priced Berncastler or Piesporter or a good Niersteiner?'

German bottle labels are most specific. There is no 'appellation contrôlée' in Germany but there are many rules and regulations that are strictly enforced and labels tell the whole story (see page 85). Here, as everywhere else, the names of the producer, shipper and importer are most important. Occasionally the name of the 'shipper' is a cleverly disguised invention by the importer himself.

You may want to serve American wines. Here the choice is less complicated because there is far less variety. You will find these wines described in some detail in the chapter on 'Wines of the United States', pp. 95-107. The best table wines of California are designated on labels by the variety of grape and the place name where the grapes were grown. You will find *Napa* and *Sonoma*, which are counties and *Livermore*, a wine-growing valley. See label on page 99.

Place names in New York State are of less significance, since practically all the wine is made in the Finger Lakes district. However, varietal names are most important. There are several native varieties and a number of hybrids—a cross of native and European grapes. The words 'Finger Lakes' are important since they designate a wine made from grapes grown in the district, not brought in from somewhere else.

Unfortunately, French names such as Burgundy, Chablis and Sauterne are used without restriction on blends and their meaning is nil or negative. These wines have little, if any, individual character.

A practice now adopted by most good producers both in California and New York State is to describe the wine in some detail in a back label. Price is a good guide with respect to quality in wines, and particularly so with American wines. The cheapest is hardly worth buying. In the east, good plain California table wines start at about $1.50 a bottle and the best will run to twice that figure. Some of the best are rarely shipped out of the State. New York State wines are about the same price.

# The Nomenclature of Wine

There are thousands and thousands of wines and each must have a name. Wine is a highly individual product. It has to be identified by those who make it, by those who take it to market and by the consumer who buys it and drinks it—and may want to talk about it later. So far, wines have not succumbed to numerical designation. Fancy ordering, in a restaurant, a fine old bottle of 764839—1947!

Wine names are place names—the place where the grapes were grown. Many food products are identified by place names—*Vermont* maple sugar, *Georgia* peaches, *Cape Cod* oysters. But the nomenclature of wine is not so simple as that. There are four gradations of place names for wine—the *region*, the *district*, the *township* (or commune) and the *vineyard*. How this breakdown works out and gives the consumer a 'handle' is best shown by the French system as it applies, for example, in the Bordeaux region.

Any wine made from grapes grown in the region in accordance with prescribed regulations can properly be called 'Bordeaux' but obviously the name is anything but specific. As a name to guide you in the choice of a wine it means very little. This is not to say that the name 'Bordeaux' is meaningless—far from it. The 'monopole' wines with 'Bordeaux' labels, bottled and shipped by highly reputable companies, will have been selected with care from wines grown in the region and

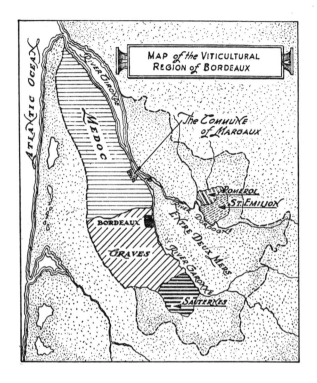

entitled to the designation, *Appellation Bordeaux Con-trôlée*.[1]

In the Bordeaux region there are several districts and the district name enables you to tell one from another. A *Graves* differs from a *Médoc* due largely to the difference in the soil of the two districts. Two other red wine districts, Saint-Emilion and Pomerol, produce

[1] Here are the names of some of the better known creators and shippers of monopoles: Barton et Gustier, Calvet, Cruse, Eschenauer, Kressmann, Schröder & Schyler, Nath. Johnston.

wines which differ slightly from one another, and both differ from a Graves or a Médoc. The *district name* tells you something of the characteristics of the wine. Though the variations may be slight, you will soon become familiar with them, and in choosing a wine to go with a dinner you may be planning, you may decide that a Saint-Emilion will be preferable to a Médoc or a Graves. And if you want a soft, velvety wine you may choose a Pomerol.

In the next gradation, proceeding from the general to the more specific, the names are not those of districts, but of *communes* in the district. The commune, in France, like the township in America, is the smallest administrative unit of government. It is not a viticultural subdivision, but wine grown within its boundaries is correctly and most usefully called by the communal name. Since the area of a commune is so small, the name is far more specific than a district name.

We now come to the highest gradation—the named vineyard. While there are in the Bordeaux *region* seven or eight *districts* and in each district from five to fifty or more *communes* there are literally thousands of named and classified vineyards. These, too, vary greatly in the quality of the wine grown. It would take the better part of a long and active wine life to get to know them all but eventually you will come to know and to recognize dozens. The infinite variety of wine is one of its fascinations. It should be remembered that a vineyard name is not, in itself, a guarantee of *quality*. It indicates only *individuality*. A district or communal wine may well be better than that of some named vineyards.

Other regions of France whose wines are imported

into this country are Burgundy, Rhône, Loire, Alsace, Jura and Provence and, of course, Champagne. In all of these regions the system of nomenclature is much the same as in Bordeaux, with the difference (of no real consequence) that in Bordeaux, almost without exception, every vineyard is called 'Château' Something-or-other. There are, of course, many venerable vineyard properties on which there is a fine old château (usually the home of the owner) but the word 'château' is a legalized adjunct of any Bordeaux vineyard name though there may be nothing more than an ordinary farmhouse on the property—or no house at all. So the word château in a Bordeaux vineyard name *may* be of no significance.

In Burgundy there are many majestic old castles (châteaux) but with only a few exceptions does the word 'château' figure in the name of the vineyard that surrounds the castle. The comparable word is *clos* (pronounced klo) which, centuries ago, designated a vineyard surrounded by stone walls, i.e. *enclosed*.

Principal *districts* in the Burgundy region are: Chablis, Côte d'Or (consisting of the Côte de Nuits and the Côte de Beaune), Mâcon and Beaujolais. Some of these district names will be found on bottle labels but most Burgundies of the Côte d'Or are called either by the names of communes or of individual vineyards. In a number of cases the name of a famous vineyard is coupled by hyphen to the original name of the commune, e.g. the commune of *Gevrey* became Gevrey-Chambertin. This is explained in the chapter on Burgundy.

Names in other French wine districts, except in

Champagne, follow a similar pattern, as will be seen in the chapters describing the wines.

The system of nomenclature in Germany is similar to the French. The districts are: Mosel (*Moselle* in both French and English), Rheingau, Rheinhesse, Rheinpfalz, Nahe and Franconia. But with the exception of Moselle the wines are not sold under district names. The district name of Rheingau is sometimes seen on bottle labels but it is there more as an additional mark of quality than as a viticultural designation. More superfine wines are grown in the Rheingau than in any of the other districts. One never sees a bottle labelled simply Rheinhesse or Rheinpfalz.

Labels without a vineyard name have the name of the township or village with the 'er' suffix added such as *Berncasteler* or *Niersteiner*. In the grade above these village or township names are the wines with vineyard names, e.g. Berncasteler, *Rosenberg*, Graacher *Himmelreich*—the vineyard in italics. But German wine labels carry much additional information about the wine in the bottle. All this is fully explained in the chapter on German wines.

In *Italy* wine names are either those of towns and villages (communes) or of grape varieties—with no apparent reason for the choice of one or the other. *Barolo*, one of the best Italian wines, is a place name—a town and township at the centre of a small district in the Piedmont. Nearby is the town of *Barbaresco* and its wine is so called. But, growing in the same area are wines called *Barbera* and *Grignolino* which are names of grape varieties.

In *Spain* wine names are those of districts with rare

reference on labels to subdivisions. The district producing the best table wines is the Rioja (ree-o-ha)—a name to look for when buying a good, every-day Spanish wine.

In the *United States*, as in Germany, there is no officially established and supervised system of nomenclature such as the Appellation Contrôlée of France. But there are a number of commendable specific regulations, both State and Federal, which have to some extent eliminated the meaningless designation seen on too many wine bottles. It is rare, if ever, that vineyard names are stated, for the obvious reason that small individual growers rarely make their grapes into wine—and certainly do not market it.

Regulations with respect to varietal names specify (in California) that a varietal must be made from at least 51 per cent of grapes of the variety named. If a district name is added the wine must be 75 per cent from the district named. If the label states 'produced and bottled by' it means that at least 51 per cent of the grapes were grown by the producer and the wine made and bottled in his winery.

# The Wine Shipper

As was stated earlier, the wine shipper is an important factor with respect to your selection of imported wines. If the bottle you hold in your hands at your wine merchant's shop, trying to decide whether to buy it or not, has on its label the name of an old and reputable shipper, that is about the best indication you can have that the wine in the bottle is an honest, sound wine.

The word 'shipper', for one who is unfamiliar with the wine trade, is something of a misnomer. The French equivalent is *négociant*, a negotiator, a trader or jobber. The prime occupation of the négociant is to select and buy wine, either at the yearly auctions or privately, and to sell in whatever market he chooses. The larger shippers have their own cellars for the storing and ageing of wine, for blending, bottling and finally packing for shipment. Many important shippers are also vineyard owners.

It is obvious that the shipper in France and in most of the wine-producing countries of Europe is the vital link between the winemaker and you, the consumer. If the shipper is a reliable House he will not put his name on a bottle of wine without knowing all about the vineyard it came from and the quality of wine grown in the year in question. He knows from long experience and close contact with the wine growers how expertly the grapes have been cultivated and harvested and made into wine.

This is specially important with respect to Burgundy,

Batard-Montrachet is the name of a small vineyard in Burgundy. Réserve des Caves de la Reine Pédauque is the shipper. The importer is Dennis & Huppert, New York.

where the land of a single famous vineyard may be the property of a number of different owners of the land, the original tract having been split up time after time by the sons and daughters who inherited it from their father. Frequently, too, in the case of large vineyards owned by the Church, the land was sold in parcels to a number of persons—often to shippers.

The competent—and usually old-established—shipper will know these individual owners and will discriminate between the good and bad. He will buy the wine (often the yield of a small strip will not be more than a few hogsheads) from the good growers, rejecting the others. He will then skilfully assemble these wines to make a sound wine in a commercially economic quantity. In many instances the small grower will not make the wine; he will sell his grapes to a shipper who will make it. The reputable shipper, loyal to a revered tradition, will know the good growers and will not bother with the others.

In addition to the name of the shipper you will find the name of the importer on the bottle—often a strip label below the wine label. This is a further guide, for, as the reputable shipper will buy and market only good wine, the high-grade importer will import only good wine.

An exception to this production and marketing system are the château wines of the Bordeaux region. Most of the great vineyards are under single ownership and their wine is made and bottled at the château, where the best of facilities for making and storage are provided. If the label on the bottle says '*Mise en bouteille au Château*', i.e. bottled at the château, you need no further guide as to *authenticity*. If the vintage is not a 'poor' year you can buy the bottle with confidence and put it gently into your cellar to age and to improve. The wine of a definitely bad year will not be bottled at the château. It will be sold in bulk and will go to market under a regional or district name as, for example, *Bordeaux Rouge*.

'Château bottled' is not, in itself, a guarantee of quality but in actual practice it is a pretty reliable indication of quality, since only a limited number of the hundreds of 'châteaux' in the Bordeaux region bottle their own wines. Those which do are pretty sure to be in the upper bracket.

# The Wines of France

France produces more wine than any other country in the world, and in particular is the largest producer of fine wines. It is the only country in which wine is a major industry. One in seven of the country's working population is engaged in it and drinks his *per capita* share—about 42 gallons a year. Italy comes close to France in production volume but makes far fewer high-quality wines and none to match France's best.

In 1964 France produced over a billion and a half gallons of table wines, roughly twenty times as much as the United States. About 15 per cent of this vast output (225 million gallons) is of quality wines and of these, in 1964, over three million gallons was imported into this country.

Wine is grown everywhere in France except in a few *Départements*[1] in the north and the greater part of it is drunk in the areas where the grapes are grown. This is *vin du pays*—the wine of the neighbouring countryside. This statement gives the correct impression of the industry but it is not strictly accurate. In a wide area stretching along the Mediterranean coast westward from the Rhône valley, are over a million acres of vines which account for more than a third of France's total production. This is flat land and rich soil; the sun is

---

[1] In 1790, following the French Revolution, the names and boundaries of the old French provinces were abolished and the country divided for administrative purposes into ninety areas called *Départements*. These correspond to counties in a State in this country, though considerably larger.

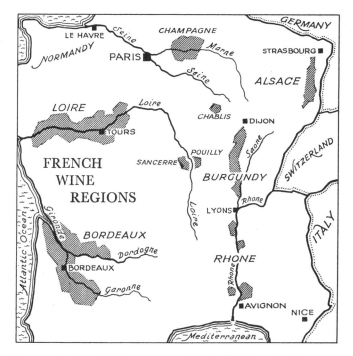

hot and the yield per acre is the highest in France.

Over 190,000 vineyard owners occupy the area but obviously all this wine is not drunk by them and their neighbours. These wines, for the most part, are *ordinaire*. Some of this vast quantity is exported in bulk, some goes into vermouth and other aperitifs and much of it is the 'pinard' drunk by the greater part of the French population.

The principal wine regions, whose product is shipped throughout the civilized world, are:

*Bordeaux*, in the south-west with the ancient city of Bordeaux at its centre.

33

*Burgundy*, a Duchy in Old France, south-east of Paris.

*Champagne*, an ancient province, 90 miles north-east of Paris.

*Rhône*, valley of the river, southward from Lyons to the Mediterranean.

*Loire*, valley stretching across central France.

*Alsace*, on the border of Germany along the west-bank of the Rhine, and a number of less important districts some of which are shown on the map.

## BORDEAUX

Of these regions, all producing fine wines, Bordeaux is the largest. It is divided into several delimited viti-cultural districts. These are the principal ones: Médoc, Graves, Saint-Emilion, Pomerol and Sauternes—see map on page 24. All these district names, and the names of communes (townships) in the districts, will be found on bottle labels. In addition there are literally hundreds of names of individual vineyards. Let us look at the characteristics of the wines in each of these districts.

*Médoc* (may-dawk)

This district, famed for its great red wines, produces a wide range—from the modest district wine, labelled simply Médoc (or more likely Haut-Médoc), to wines as fine as any in the world. Those with names of communes which you will find in most well-stocked wine shops in this country are: Margaux, delicate; St Julien, rather more body, and St Estèphe, full-bodied. Another very important commune is Pauillac where are grown many of the finest red wines of France.

In the quality scale above these are the classified growths, or *Crus*. Cru means simply a vineyard property. In the official classification there are five grades of quality. In the first grade—*Premiers Crus*—are the super wines—*Château Margaux, Château Lafite-Rothschild* and *Château Latour*. These are not wines that you and I will drink very often. They cost too much—not only because of their superior excellence but due to their rarity in any given market throughout the world. In the four other growths, the second, third, fourth and fifth, are sixty named vineyards. Here are a dozen of them, taken at random. Following these are some 250 lesser growths all of which yield excellent wines, though of less distinction.

Second Growths: *Ch. Lascombes, Ch. Montrose, Ch. Léoville-Poyferré.*

Third Growths: *Ch. Calon-Ségur, Ch. Palmer, Ch. La Lagune.*

Fourth Growths: *Ch. Talbot, Ch. Pierre Bontemps, Ch. Beychevelle.*

Fifth Growths: *Ch. Pontet Canet,*[1] *Ch. Lynch-Bages, Ch. Cantemerle.*

**1411329**

*Graves* (graave—drop the 's')

This district grows both red and white wines but it is chiefly the white that you will find in most wine shops. However, there is one notable exception, the world

[1] Château Pontet Canet is never château bottled. This venerable vineyard is the property of Cruse et Fils Frères and the wine is taken to their cellars in Bordeaux and bottled there. This in no way diminishes its quality or its high standard.

renowned *Château Haut-Brion*. This extraordinary wine
is officially classed with the three First Growths of the
Médoc. The ancient vineyard once belonged to Talley-
rand but for some years has been the property of Mr
Clarence Dillon, the New York banker. Alongside
Haut-Brion is *Château La Mission Haut-Brion*, producing
a delightful, rather delicate red wine. Other red wines of
the Graves: *Château Bouscaut, Château Pape Clément,
Château Smith-Haut-Lafite*.

The wines of the Graves, especially the white wines,
have a distinctive taste which comes from the gravelly
soil of the district; in fact the name derives from the
French word *gravier* which means gravel. No other

white wine of France is quite like it. I find it agreeable and a pleasant change occasionally from, for example, the ordinary white wine of Mâcon. But no Graves can match the superior white wines of the Côte d'Or. A few of the better white Graves that you will find in many wine shops are: *Château Bouscaut, Château Carbonnieux, Château Couhins, Château Laville Haut-Brion, Château Olivier*. Normally these wines will be 'château bottled'. A bottle labelled simply 'Graves', unless followed by the words 'Appellation Contrôlée', should be rejected.

*Saint-Emilion* (San-tay-meel-yon)

This is a famous red wine district—no white wine of any consequence. The name is known to wine lovers everywhere and the popularity of its wines is well merited.

37

Their general level of quality is higher than that of any other Bordeaux district (except Pomerol), which is to say that a plain Saint-Emilion may well be a bit better than a plain Médoc or Graves. The district lies about 20 miles east of the city of Bordeaux and its vines cover some 16,000 acres. Saint-Emilion is extensively imported into this country; you will find it in most wine shops.

These wines are in general rather fuller bodied than those of the Médoc. They have been called the 'Burgundies of Bordeaux'. Whether the proud wine makers of Burgundy go along with this analogy is another matter. At any rate the wines are excellent and the range of quality so wide that anyone will find a Saint-Emilion to his liking which he can afford to enjoy frequently. A bottle ticketed simply 'Saint-Emilion— Appellation Contrôlée' will contain a wine that will be pretty sure to please, and the price will be reasonable.

When you want something very much better, it is available in large measure. The really super Saint-Emilions are classified in two grades: *Great First Growths* and *Great Growths*—twelve of the former and thirty of the latter. At the zenith of the Great First Growths is *Château Ausone* (oh-zone), an extraordinary wine. The name is derived from Ausonius, the Roman poet who was born in Bordeaux (*c.* 310) and who planted a vineyard in the district in the first half of the fourth century. Next to *Ausone*, and perhaps its equal, is *Château Cheval Blanc* (White Horse) and after that come the remaining ten Great Firsts.

The thirty Great Growths follow, and here are the names of half a dozen of them: *Château Bellevue, Château*

*Chauvin, Château Coutet, Château Grand-Corbin, Château la Carte* and *Château Grand Mayne.*

Adjacent to the central commune, Saint-Emilion, are seven smaller communes all of which are legally entitled to the name Saint-Emilion. Most of these wines are so much like those of the parent commune that only an expert could tell the difference. Slightly further removed are six secondary communes whose wines are designated by the name of the commune *linked by hyphen to Saint-Emilion.*

These names, which you are apt to find on wine-shop shelves and restaurant wine lists, are:

*Saint-Georges-Saint-Emilion, Montagne-Saint Emilion, Lussac-Saint-Emilion, Puisseguin-Saint-Emilion, Parsac-Saint-Emilion* and *Sables-Saint-Emilion.*

In these six communes are 215 named vineyards and in the rest of the district nearly 1,000 more.

*Pomerol* (paum-may-rawl)

With a tenth the acreage of Saint-Emilion, which it adjoins, this is a perfect gem of a wine district. Its wines are excellent and their average quality higher than in Saint-Emilion. The district wine labelled simply 'Pomerol' will usually be superior to any other district wine of the Bordeaux region, and more dependable.

There is one exceptional wine, that of the *Château Petrus.* It ranks with the *Premier Crus* of the Médoc and with *Ausone* and *Cheval Blanc* of Saint-Emilion. This is the bottle to serve when you want to impress a connoisseur who is coming to dinner. There are seventeen other upper-bracket Pomerols: here are a few of them: *Château Certan, Château Vieux Château Certan*—two unrelated vineyards in spite of the similarity of their names—*Château La Conseillante, Château L'Evangile, Château La Fleur, Château Beauregard, Château Gazin, Château Nenin, Château La Pointe.*

*Sauternes* (so-tairne—drop the 's')

Here is a wine district, producing possibly the finest natural sweet wines of the world, and whose name has been singularly abused—particularly in this country. More later on this aspect of the matter; suffice it to say here that the so-called 'Sauterne', spelled without the final 's' and mispronounced *saw-turn*, is not in any sense a counterpart of the Sauternes of France. These are superlative dessert wines. Served with the sweet course, they climax a perfect dinner; are a compliment to the host and a delight to his guests.

The district, called in French the *Sauternais* (so-tair-nay), lies at the southern tip of the Bordeaux region. There are five communes: Sauternes itself, the largest, Barsac, Preignac, Bommes and Fargues. Some 4,000 acres are planted to vines and there are about 300 named vineyards. The wine of Barsac is called by the communal name but that of the other four is designated Sauternes. Most of the better grades will carry the vineyard name and many are château-bottled.

In the official classification there is one, and only one, *First Great Growth—Château d'Yquem* (dee-kem), known throughout the world. Due to its super excellence and its scarcity it is rather costly. Here are the names of a half dozen châteaux of the classified *First* and *Second Growths*, any of which you can serve most acceptably instead of the First and only '*Great*'.

40

First Growths: *Château Guiraud, Château La Tour Blanche, Château Coutet, Château Climens, Château Rieussec, Château Suduiraut.*

Second Growths: *Château Filhot, Château Lamothe, Château d'Arche, Château Myrat, Château Caillou, Château de Malle.*

Why are the Sauternes so sweet? This and other characteristics which make the wine so attractive are due in part to the nature of the soil but not largely to this influence. As the grapes become ripe a curious mould forms on the skin of the berries and sucks water from the juice. This mould is formed by a parasite called *Botrytis cinerea*, present in the district.[1] In addition to depriving the grape of its natural water-sugar balance—increasing the amount of sugar—it brings about minute changes in the constitution of the juice. When this mould starts to work the berries begin to shrivel and a kind of decay sets in. This is called *pourriture noble* (noble rot)—a pleasant euphemism.

When the grapes are quite shrivelled and have lost much of their water they are gathered almost one by one. Since only those berries which have reached this state are wanted for pressing, the gathering of the grapes is a meticulous and costly business. The vines are searched for berries deeply affected by the mould and these are snipped from the bunches with long thin scissors. Before the harvest is completed the vines may be gone over several times to glean the grapes that are

[1] The *Botrytis cinerea* occurs also in some of the vineyards of the Rhine and Moselle valleys in Germany. Here it is called Edelfäule (aydel-foy-l'uh) and the resulting wine, made as in Sauternes, is called *Trockenbeerenauslese*. These wines, too, are very costly—a single bottle may cost as much as $40 even in Germany.

Sauternes grapes affected by the 'noble rot'.

fit for the great wine they are to yield from the fermentation vats.

Fermentation takes place in the usual manner but
owing to the excess of sugar it ceases when the concen-
tration of alcohol reaches 13 to 15 per cent. At this
alcoholic strength the finished wine still contains a
substantial amount of sugar. That is why and how
Sauternes is sweet. This degree of sugar, like the sugar
in jam, permits the wine to 'keep' well even after the
cork has been drawn.

A dessert wine is served in small glasses along with the
sweets and if there are no more than four at table the
bottle will remain half full. No harm; put it in the
refrigerator for the next special occasion.

B U R G U N D Y — Bourgogne in French (boor-gon-yuh)

This region, once a Duchy ruled by the Dukes of Bourgogne, is smaller in area than Bordeaux and its total wine production about one-third that of Bordeaux. But Burgundy grows a large number of exceptionally fine wines.

The region begins at Dijon, 200 miles south-east of Paris, and extends southward for 100 miles, almost to the city of Lyons. All of the super wines of the region—those that come to mind when Burgundy is mentioned—are grown in the northern district, the *Côte d'Or* (Golden Slope). Those in the top grade are unsurpassed by any other wines of the world. The great red Burgundies are the ideal accompaniment of game and a fine roast of beef. Both red and white wines are grown—more red than white.

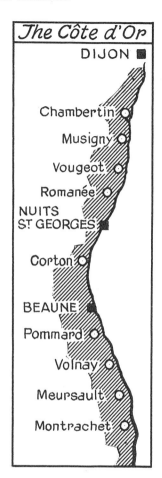

The Côte d'Or

DIJON

Chambertin

Musigny

Vougeot

Romanée

NUITS ST GEORGES

Corton

BEAUNE

Pommard

Volnay

Meursault

Montrachet

43

Here are the names of a few of the most renowned red wines: *Chambertin*, often, and justifiably, qualified the most famous red wine of the world; *Clos de Bèze*, whose vineyards are contiguous with *Chambertin*, often matches its illustrious neighbour in quality though not in fame; *Romanée-Conti*, a world-famous vineyard of just over four acres; *Les Grands Echézeaux*, *Le Musigny*, *La Tache*, *Corton*. All of these are red wines but *Corton* grows also one of the finest white wines. The famous white wines, in order of excellence: *Montrachet*, *Corton-Charlemagne*, *Meursault-Perrières*.

Many excellent wines of the Côte d'Or are bottled under the names of communes. In the Côte de Nuits— *Gevrey-Chambertin*, *Morey-Saint-Denis*, *Vougeot*, *Vosne-Romanée*, *Nuits-Saint-Georges*. In the Côte de Beaune— *Pommard*, *Volnay*, *Chassagne-Montrachet*, *Meursault* and *Puligny-Montrachet*. If they come from a reliable shipper via an equally reliable importer, and if the label carries the words 'Appellation Contrôlée', you can buy the bottle with complete assurance. These communal wines will be much lower in price than many of those with vineyard names.

Here it is necessary to explain the wine growing and marketing practices of the Burgundy region (in particular those of the Côte d'Or) which differ radically from those of Bordeaux and other regions. The basic difference arises from the fact that the great vineyards of the Côte d'Or are, in many cases, not under single ownership. For example, the 32 acres of the thirteen-hundred-year-old vineyard of Chambertin, and its adjoining vineyard, Clos de Bèze (37 acres), are divided among twenty or more individual owners. The famous

Château of the Clos de Vougeot—fourteenth century.

vineyard of the venerable Clos de Vougeot, once the property of the Cistercian Monks, with 124 acres of vines, is now owned by some sixty different growers.[1]

These great vineyards were originally under single ownership, either a venerable wine-growing family, a monastery or a convent. The privately owned vineyard, at the death of the owner, was divided amongst his children. If there were four legatees the vineyard was divided into four plots or parcels. After even two or three generations these parcels had become quite small. In some rare cases one of the legatees did not want to follow in his father's footsteps; he sold his parcel to an outsider—often to a négociant. The vineyards of the Church suffered the same fate. And so began the break-up, *as to ownership*, of many of the great properties. The famous name is preserved and all the wine from all the

[1] This property, along with all feudal estates, was expropriated by the Government following the French Revolution. It remained State property for 100 years but was then sold (in 1891) to fifteen individual buyers.

45

parcels, made by all of the different owners, is entitled to the great name. It will be obvious that not every bottle labelled Chambertin or Clos de Vougeot will be identical.

Many of these individual small owners have neither the capital nor the facilities for making the wine, much less for marketing it. In many cases the yield is far too small. So they sell their wine either privately or at auction to a négociant. The Burgundy auctions are famous and attended by buyers from many countries. The buyer takes the wine to his own cellars for ageing, blending and marketing. To obtain a commercial quantity of a given wine he may buy it from perhaps a half dozen grower-owners.

But not all of the growers are equally skilled and conscientious; and here is where the standing of the négociant becomes so important to the eventual consumer. If he has built up a good reputation he will want to sustain it and he will buy his parcels of grapes or wine only from the good growers. He knows them all and can easily accumulate only good, sound wines.

So much for the great Côte d'Or.

## MACON

Southward is the *Mâconnais* (mac-con-nay), with the town of Mâcon at its centre, and further on is the Beaujolais (bo-jo-lay). As you travel, either by road or rail, from Paris to Lyons on your way to the Rivièra, along the right bank of the Saône (sône), which joins the Rhône at Lyons, the vineyards will be seen on your right. Two districts, Mâcon and Beaujolais, are generally considered to be a part of the Burgundy region but

few of their wines are sold as 'Burgundy'. Legally they can be, but in practice Mâcon is sold as Mâcon and Beaujolais as Beaujolais—a name almost as well known as Burgundy. Either of these districts grows more wine than the whole of the Côte d'Or—but none comes anywhere near the Côte d'Or's best.

The Mâconnais produces both red and white wine and both have a characteristic taste that is easily distinguishable once you get to know it. It is not easy to describe—the best thing to do is to try them. When I buy a couple of cases of 'everyday' wine I like to include a mixed case of red and white Mâcon, e.g. Mâcon Blanc Supérieur and a Mâcon Supérieur Rouge. In London, where I am writing these lines, they cost about $1.50 a bottle. They will be a bit higher in the U.S.

There is no red Mâcon of distinction but there are

white Mâcons that rank with the lesser Growths of Mersault and Chablis. The best white wine comes from the *village* of Pouilly in the *commune* of Fuissé. This wine, of which the yield is small, is properly called *Pouilly Fuissé*, but here is another case, like so many in the Côte d'Or, where a fine wine, due to its excellence, has been called upon to lend its lustre to the wine of its neighbours. The wines of three adjoining communes go to market as Pouilly-Fuissé. These are the communes of *Solutré*, *Vergisson* and *Chaintré*. Thus, four prolific communes contribute to the supply of wine sold under the very well-known name of Pouilly-Fuissé. Some of these may match the quality of the wine of the village of Pouilly but certainly not all of them.

To make sure of getting one of the better ones look for the vineyard name. The best vineyard name at Pouilly is *Le Clos* and another good one (in Fuissé) is *Château Fuissé*. In Solutré is *Le Mont Garcin*, in Vergisson *Les Charmes* and in Chaintré *Le Paradis*.[1] Any of these, and of other named vineyards, are likely to be a bit better than a simple Pouilly-Fuissé. You may not want to be this fussy about it, though I think this sort of searching is fascinating. In the *six* communes producing the superior white wines of Mâcon are two—also contiguous with Fuissé—whose wines are *not* called Pouilly-Fuissé. These are *Loché* and *Vinzelles*. But the magic name of Pouilly, which is about two miles away, *is* used. Their wines are called Pouilly-Loché and Pouilly-Vinzelles. They are about the equal of the Pouilly-Fuissés. So, it appears that the little village of Pouilly effectively dominates the

---

[1] André Simon's suggestion in his *Noble Grapes and Great Wines of France*. McGraw-Hill, 1957.

nomenclature of this renowned fine white-wine district.[1]

## BEAUJOLAIS

We come now to the famous district of Beaujolais which adjoins Mâcon on the south. The wine-growing area, about the same size as that of Mâcon, produces almost three times as much wine—some 14 million gallons, mostly red. The cultivation of the vine far surpasses that of any other crop. Even so, the worldwide demand for Beaujolais may sometimes exceed the supply and what is lacking may come from other sources. However, these spurious wines are unlikely to reach this country.

Beaujolais is an attractive name and this may in part account for its great popularity. It was perhaps for this reason that, thirty years ago, I was inclined to downgrade Beaujolais as a very ordinary wine—in any case, not one to be served to one's friends. That was a mistake. Certainly there are some pretty ordinary Beaujolais but there are many very good ones. The wine is fresh and fruity and can be drunk when quite young. It is often 'ready' when six months old, and at its best before its second birthday. It goes well with almost any food. Every regular wine drinker should have a few bottles of Beaujolais in his cellar.

· Beaujolais is *the* wine of the restaurants in the city of Lyons—only 20 miles distant, where it is stocked in cask

---

[1] To make this whole Pouilly business even more complicated, there is a *Pouilly Fumé* in the Loire valley 100 miles away. 'Fumé' is not a commune but the name of the variety of grape from which the wine is made, *Blanc Fumé*, the local name for the renowned Sauvignon of Bordeaux.

and served in a pitcher or carafe. This applies only in less degree to the popular restaurants and bistros of Paris. I used to frequent a restaurant in the Avenue Marceau, called Ramponneau (excellent cuisine), and the wine waiter, in his blue denim smock, always came to my table as soon as I had ordered the food and would ask '*Quel est votre menu?*' What have you ordered? When I had told him he would almost invariably suggest '*Un petit pichet de Beaujolais*', a little pitcher of Beaujolais—no matter what food I had chosen—and usually I took his advice. No doubt Ramponneau's cellars housed many large casks of Beaujolais.

There are two categories of 'district' wines: *Beaujolais* and *Beaujolais Supérieur*. Both are official *appellations*, controlled by the National Institute of Appellations of Origin. The wine must be made from grapes grown within the legal limits of the Beaujolais district. Plain Beaujolais must have at least 9 per cent of alcohol

BEAUJOLAIS
VILLAGES
1964

APPELLATION CONTRÔLÉE          NICOLAS. CHARENTON-SEINE

and the yield cannot exceed roughly 540 gallons per acre; Beaujolais Supérieur—alcohol 10 per cent and yield 480 gallons. In the category above these two district appellations are *Beaujolais Villages* and wines labelled Beaujolais followed by the name of the vineyard or controlled area in which the grapes were grown, e.g. '*Beaujolais-Brouilly*'. Permitted yield 430 gallons per acre. Obviously, the quality of the wine rises as the regulations become more stringent.

The wine of thirty-five communes is entitled to one or the other of the foregoing designations. In the top class are nine wine districts whose limits are fixed by A.O.C. regulations. These are the names to look for when you want the best of Beaujolais. Here they are: *Moulin-à-Vent* (windmill), *Fleurie, Juliénas, Morgon* (or *Villié-Morgon*), *Brouilly, Côte de Brouilly, Chiroubles, Chénas, Saint-Amour*.

These sound like names of vineyard properties but they are not. Some are names of communes, others of small areas designated by the A.O.C. It is not easy to place these wines in an order of quality; all are good. *Moulin-à-Vent* is often considered rather the best of all, but you can decide that for yourself.

## CHABLIS

Eighty-five miles south-east of Paris, about half-way to Dijon, where the traditional Burgundy wine region begins, is the small district of Chablis (shab-lee) from which comes a delightful, pale green, dry, white wine. The fame of this wine has made the name Chablis known throughout the world and, like Sauternes, it is greatly abused. A lot of wine grown in this country,

Alcohol Content :
12,5% by Volume

Net Contents :
1 Pint 8 Fl. OZS

WHITE BURGUNDY

## PETIT CHABLIS
APPELLATION CONTROLÉE

Produced and Bottled by : *Collin & Bourissel*
*WINE MERCHANTS AT MACON FRANCE*

Imported by : DENNIS & HUPPERT Inc., 1790 Broadway
NEW-YORK 19 N. Y.                    Permit N° 2-1-578

both in California and in New York State, goes to market under a label which says it is Chablis. It is legal for any wine maker to apply the name to any white wine of whatever origin.[1] Some of these wines are not bad, but if you are familiar with the true Chablis of France you probably will find little resemblance except as to colour.

A good many of the lesser wines of the Chablis district are quite ordinary but they are identifiable by their label and are at least authentic. They must be made from the same variety of grape, the Chardonnay, as are the higher grade wines and the legal designation for them is *Petit Chablis*—Little Chablis. Most of this wine is consumed either locally or in Paris bistros where it is drawn from the cask and served *en carafe* or in little brown pitchers (pee-shay).
country.

The finest Chablis is produced in seven named vine-

[1] It can be from any variety of vine or combination of varieties, and from any district in the region. But the label must make it clear that it is not French, e.g. California Chablis, New York Chablis.

yards, officially called *Grands Crus*—Great Growths. These wines will be so labelled and some of them will be 'estate bottled'.

These seven vineyards cover only about 90 acres and the permitted yield averages 400 gallons per acre. Since this volume must respond to the world demand it is obvious that these top quality wines will be rare and rather costly. Here are the names of the seven vineyards: *Blanchots, Bougros, Les Clos, Grenouilles* (meaning frogs), *Les Preuses, Valmur* and *Vaudésir*. These are top Chablis —and very good wines they are. By common consent among experts, Chablis is the ideal wine with oysters, but of course you can do very well with the second category—*Premier Crus*—First Growths. There is also a third category entitled to the simple appellation *Chablis*, and finally, *Petit Chablis* (puh-tee), as mentioned above.

The regulations of the Appellation d'Origine Contrôlée hold a tight rein over these properties. All Chablis wines must be made from the Chardonnay grape and the permitted yield and minimum alcoholic strength is stipulated. Grand Cru maximum yield 375 gallons per acre, minimum alcohol $10\frac{1}{2}$ per cent; Premier Cru and Chablis 425 gallons and 10 per cent alcohol; Petit Chablis, 425 gallons, alcohol $9\frac{1}{2}$ per cent.

You will have no problem when you go to buy a bottle, or a case, of upper-bracket Chablis. The labels tell you the whole story. They will carry the name of the vineyard and/or the name of the commune. A *Grand Cru* Chablis of a good year, 1962 for example, will be priced at around $4.25 and a *Premier Cru* at only a little less. A 'Chablis' Cru may be had for about $3.

## THE RHÔNE

Two great rivers of Western Europe are the Rhine and the Rhône. Both have their source in Switzerland but they soon part company. The Rhine flows north, the Rhône south. The Rhine is majestic, the Rhône awesome. I have a soft spot for the Rhône; my ancestors came from the valley over two centuries ago. The Rhône is not only awesome; some stretches of it are frightening. None but a strong swimmer would dare try to cross it lest he be carried to his death by the swift current.

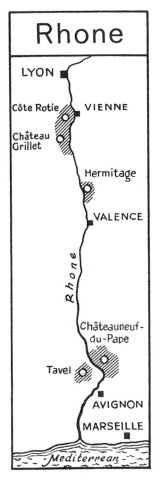

Some great and good wines are grown in the Rhône Valley—wines that have much historical interest, wines that age well and improve with time.

From the city of Lyons the Rhône flows directly south to the Mediterranean and along its banks are three groups of vineyards, with wide gaps between them. The first group lies about 20 miles below Lyons and is called Côte Rotie (roasted

54

slope). Here some of the best Rhône wines are grown. Most of them are marketed as *Côte Rotie* and bottles so labelled are found in the wine shops of this country.

Côte Rotie is under the regulation of the Appellation Contrôlée and you should make sure that these words are on the label. The entire yearly production of the district does not exceed 30,000 gallons.

Adjoining Côte Rotie on the south is *Condrieu* (cawn-dree-uh), a still smaller section in which only white wine is grown. From one of these vineyards, the *Château Grillet* (gree-yay), comes the recognized best white wine of the Rhône. There are only 3 acres in Château Grillet, yielding some 400 gallons a year. Not many bottles of this fine wine will be found in the United States. Most of it is drunk within 25 miles of the vineyard in two famous restaurants nearby.[1]

South of Condrieu and after a gap of 20 miles are the vineyards of Hermitage (air-me-taj) which, though small in acreage, are known throughout the world. Mention Rhône wines to wine lovers anywhere and nine out of ten will think first of Hermitage. These vineyards are terraced on steep slopes much like those of the Moselle valley in Germany.

Hermitage grows stout wines, rough when young but which mellow and mature with age as well as or better than many of the other red wines of France. They spend the first two years of their life in cask, throwing a heavy deposit. When racked and bottled at the end of this brief adolescence they are clean and smooth but they will further improve for another five or ten years. When you find a Hermitage that is ten or fifteen years old you

[1] La Pyramide at Vienne and Pic at Valence.

PRODUCT OF FRANCE
ALCOHOL 18°/, BY VOLUME    CONTENTS 1 PINT 8"FL. OZ.
TRADE    MARK

TAVEL

ROSÉ

APPELLATION CONTRÔLÉE

PAUL JABOULET AÎNÉ

TAIN (DRÔME) FRANCE

may consider yourself fortunate. Crozes-Hermitage (crows) is a district which surrounds Hermitage except for its river frontage. Its wines, though similar to Hermitage, are not quite as good.

Hermitage produces white wines as well. These, too, are rough when young but like the reds they age well—better than most of the white wines of France. There are *named vineyard areas*, but the names are rarely used on bottle labels.

Below Hermitage is another and longer gap and at its end are the southernmost Rhône vineyards, much more extensive than Côte Rotie and Hermitage put together. Here is grown another world-famous wine, Châteauneuf du Pape (the Pope's new Château), a glamorous name that surely is a great commercial asset.

Châteauneuf du Pape is made from many varieties of grape crushed and mixed together in the fermenting vats. By law, in order to enjoy the benefit (which is great) of Appellation Contrôlée, the wine must have an alcohol content of at least $12\frac{1}{2}$ per cent. The wine is full bodied and, though of slightly higher alcoholic strength, is lighter than some of those of the Côte Rotie and matures faster than Hermitage. Owing to the far greater volume of production, it is also lower in price.

You are unlikely to find bottles of Châteauneuf du Pape from named vineyards but if you want to search for one, here are the names of a few: *Château Fortia, Château des Fines Roches, Château de la Nerthe, Château de Vaudieu, Château Rayas.*

The other famous wine of the district comes from the commune of Tavel across the river. Tavel is often credited with being the finest *rosé* of France, and that is to say, of the world. It is certainly the best known. It is made mostly from one variety of grape, the Grenache (gren-ash), and by the first-mentioned method described in a previous chapter on rosé, i.e. removing the skins and seeds from the fermenting *must* before too much colour has been imparted to the wine. This, as has been said, does not in any way diminish its eventual alcoholic content—from 12 to 14 per cent. The vines grow in a thin sandy soil and the yield per acre is below average, which accounts for the delightful charm and flavour of the wine.

The commune of Lirac, adjoining Tavel on the north, produces a rosé much like Tavel and if you find one it may cost less since it is, by comparison, little known.

## THE LOIRE

The wine region of the Loire (lwahr) is extensive both as to the acreage of its vineyards and its volume of production, but it is secondary to Bordeaux and Burgundy in importance. Its vineyards lie along the banks of the river Loire, France's longest and most beautiful river. Though its source is less than 100 miles from the Mediterranean, it has scorned the watershed that directs the Rhône southward and makes for the Atlantic 600 miles away. Along its winding course are several distinct wine districts with a vast total acreage of vines.

White wines predominate by a wide margin though the great and growing popularity of pink wine has led to the production of a lot of rosé. Most of the white wines, both still and sparkling, are on the sweet side but few can be called great. On the whole they are simply agreeable, light wines, fresh and fruity with nothing of the character of the great white wines of Burgundy and the Rhine. Some of the sparkling wines are claimed to be second only to Champagne—and possibly they are— but make no mistake, they are not a close second.

By far the best dry wines of the Loire are those of two relatively small areas—*Pouilly-sur-Loire* and *Sancerre*. The name to look for when you want the best Pouilly is *Pouilly-Fumé*, or *Pouilly-Blanc-Fumé*. This wine is made from the great white-wine grape, the Sauvignon, locally called Blanc-Fumé.[1] It is important to remember this, for three-fifths of the wine of Pouilly-sur-Loire, labelled plain *Pouilly*, is made from an inferior variety of grape. This caution is not needed with Sancerre because the only grape grown there is the Blanc-Fumé.

For top quality of Pouilly-Blanc-Fumé, look for labels with village or communal names. Vineyard names on labels are rare. There is one château at Pouilly, the *Château de Nozet*. As to Sancerre, there is also

[1] Fumé means smoked, but its origin as the name of a vine is obscure. At any rate the wine is not smoky or smoked.

one château, the *Château de Sancerre*. Other wines may carry on their labels the names of small villages: *Bué*, *Chavignol*, *Amigny*, *Verdigny*, coupled, of course, with the word *Sancerre*.

A point to remember about Pouilly Fumé is that it has no relation to the better known Pouilly Fuissé of the Mâconnais (see page 48). Both are excellent wines and their general characteristics are similar, but there is a difference due to the variety of grape. Pouilly Fuissé is more widely available in this country.

There is one other dry wine, called *Muscadet*, grown far down the river, near its mouth at Nantes. It is made from the *Muscadet* grape. Light and fruity, it has won some popularity in the past decade or two. It is perhaps the lowest in price of any dry white French wine available in this country. A fact to keep in mind is that Muscadet is in no way related to *Muscatel*, a grape grown almost everywhere in the world and which normally yields a sweet wine.

The best known and most widely available Loire wines are those of *Vouvray* (voo-vray), *Saumur* (so-muhr) and *Anjou* (ahn-joo). These are the ones alluded to earlier—the agreeable light wines altogether suitable as luncheon wines. None is distinguished. Many are sparkling—fermented in bottle like champagne. Owing to the tax on all sparkling wines, good and bad, they are rather high in price—often approaching the cost of non-vintage French Champagne and of the better California and New York Champagnes.

Perhaps the most distinguished wine of the Loire— the one which holds its own with the fine Sauternes—is a sweet wine called *Quarts de Chaume* (car-duh-shome),

one of a group of vineyards along the banks of a small tributary, the Layon, which joins the Loire not far from its mouth in the Atlantic. In good years Quarts de Chaume is an exquisite dessert wine. Another of the same character is *Bonnezeaux* (bonne-ay-zo). It is less well known and may be hard to find in the wine shops.

Two red wines of the Loire should be mentioned—*Bourgeuil* and *Chinon*, the former of fuller body and usually labelled St Nicolas-de-Bourgeuil.

## ALSACE

The wine region in Alsace lies between the west bank of the river Rhine and the foothills of the Vosges mountains. It is a narrow strip extending from Strasbourg to Mulhouse—a distance of 60 miles. This is ancient wine country, dating from the first century A.D. Here 30,000 acres of white wine grapes yield some 25 million gallons of wine a year. Of this total production about two-fifths is drunk in the homes and cafés of

Alsace and Lorraine; a like amount is sent to other parts of France, chiefly Paris, and much of the remainder is exported to Great Britain and the United States. Imports into this country have increased greatly in the past 20 years. In 1965 they were some 40,000 gallons.

These are dry wines—some of them very dry—and they resemble to some extent their near neighbours in Germany. They come in tall green bottles, like the Moselles. They are less delicate and the alcohol content is higher—from 10 to 13 per cent. They are more robust than the Moselles and most of them have a flowery and fruity flavour. They stand up well to the rich pâtés and sausages for which Alsace is famous. There are many excellent Alsatian restaurants in Paris, and, of course, all serve the wine of Alsace.

Unlike other wines of France, Alsace only rarely designates its wines by place names. They take the name of the grape from which they are made. Following the return of Alsace to France in 1918 the low-grade, high-yield vines which had been planted by the Germans

61

were uprooted and replaced by superior varieties. Varietal names were then adopted to show that these good vines were now restored. The best of these is the *Riesling* and the wine of this noble grape is proudly so ticketed, as you will see from the label reproduced. Some growers couple the place name with the name of the grape, e.g. *Riesling de Riquewihr* (reek-veer) and *Riesling de Ribeauvillé* (ree-bo-vee-lay), the second word being that of the place of origin. In this way the grower distinguishes *his* Riesling from a wine labelled simply 'Alsace Riesling', which could come from anywhere in Alsace. Riquewihr, Ribeauvillé and two or three other villages have a reputation for superior wines. So it can be taken for granted that when the origin is thus specified the wine in the bottle will likely be of better quality and higher in price. Vineyard names are seldom used.

Another quality grape is the Traminer (tra-meen-er) and a sub variety, called Gewürztraminer, which is put forward as rather special, and the wine costs more. About the only difference between the two is that the wine of the latter has a distinctly spicey flavour. gewürz (guh-voortz) is the German word for spice. A third variety, widely planted, is the *Sylvaner* (sil-vanner), a high-yield vine whose wine has little distinction. It is an agreeable luncheon wine and goes well as an after dinner beverage to while away the evening. Most Alsatian wines, bearing varietal names, are made from that one grape alone, but there are blends. These must be labelled *Zwicker* and they should cost less.

Wine making in Alsace is in an advanced state and great care is exercised by all the better growers. The grapes are crushed; then they are squeezed in pneumatic presses. This method leaves little or no foreign matter in the must, and consequently the wine 'falls bright' after its slow fermentation. A single racking is usually all that is necessary. The wine is kept in wooden casks for eight months or so and is then bottled and ready for drinking.

## CHAMPAGNE

Champagne, that sparkling French wine that everybody knows and most persons greatly enjoy, is the ideal all-purpose wine. You serve it as an aperitif before lunch or dinner, or all through a meal as the only wine. If other wines accompany the food, Champagne will provide the final climax if served with the sweet. No other bottle brought to the table will so delight your guests. And quite apart from any connection with mealtime, Champagne is the wine for congratulations and good wishes on any occasion. And it is *the* wine for the sick, the invalid and the convalescent. Champagne is one of France's major accomplishments.

Sorting *Champagne* grapes at the roadside.
*Photo courtesy of Lanson père et fils.*

Champagne gets its name from the old Province of Champagne. It owes its excellence to three things; the extremely chalky soil of the region, the quality of the noble Pinot grape,[1] and the skill, care and patience with which the wine is made.

The Champagne district lies some 90 miles to the north-east of Paris. The city of Reims (pronounced *ranz*, spelled Rheims in English) is its commercial centre. Another important Champagne town is Epernay. Within this legally delimited area, 25,000–30,000 acres

[1] There are, in fact, two varieties of Pinot, the *Pinot noir* and the *Chardonnay*. In Champagne the Pinot noir predominates to the extent of 80 per cent. These are wine grapes of exceptional quality. All the great red Burgundies of the Côte d'Or are made from the Pinot noir.

of vines are owned and cultivated by some 16,000 individual growers. No wine made in France, though it sparkle ever so enticingly, can be labelled Champagne unless made from grapes grown in this district.

Champagne is not a 'natural' wine in the sense that it is not the result of natural fermentation alone as are the still wines. It is a 'made' wine—a blend of wines from many vineyards, and the process by which it is produced is complicated. In Champagne there is no celebrated vineyard to extol. No Champagne is ever 'château bottled'. The all-important name is that of the House that produces it, e.g. Bollinger, Clicquot, Irroy, Krug, Lanson, Moët et Chandon, Mercier, Mumm, Pommery-Greno, Roederer. There are many others.

The production process is like this. Except for the growing and harvesting of the grapes the making of Champagne is in the hands of the great and lesser Houses who buy the grapes from the vineyard owners.[1] These vineyardists (*vignerons*—veen-yer-awn) gather their grapes and inspect them at the nearest roadside, carefully examining each bunch for defective berries and snipping them out with long, thin scissors. With this the grower's share of the work is finished.

The House which has bought the grapes collects them and promptly takes them to the nearest press house (*pressoir*—press-whar). It is desirable that the grapes be pressed as soon as possible after being taken from the vines. Some of the larger companies have their own presshouses in a number of villages. These presses, made of oak, will handle four tons of grapes at a time.

---

[1] Some of the larger Houses have their own vineyards but buy as well from the individual growers.

Blending of parcels of wine from different vineyards.
*Photo courtesy of Lanson père et fils.*

The grapes are not previously crushed as with other wines because the skins of the black grapes would quickly impart their colour to the juice. The bunches of grapes are tipped from their wicker baskets on to the floor of the press, the great oak cover is screwed down and the grapes are gently squeezed.

The juice flows freely through the open-work sides of the press into deep grooves or troughs which carry it to a collection tank. It starts fermenting at once and in this active state is hauled in tank trucks to the processing plant of the House that bought the grapes. On arrival it is transferred to large glass-lined vats where it will continue its first and natural fermentation. This will take

Rémuage. *Photo courtesy of Lanson père et fils.*

eight to ten weeks. The new wine is then racked, i.e. drawn off from its lees into clean casks or blending vats.

By the end of the harvest there will be a large number of these parcels of wine from different vineyards, each lot fermenting in its own vat and each differing a little from the others. These wines are now blended to form a single wine from each locality. This 'assembled' wine is now put in casks or vats for a further rest of four or five weeks where it usually will continue a slow fermentation.

At the final racking in late winter the various assembled wines are blended by the *Chef de Caves* (caave) (Chief of the Cellars) and thoroughly mixed in

67

large vessels. This now homogeneous wine is ready for bottling and receives a dose of syrup made from cane sugar dissolved in wine. This will ensure the necessary further fermentation in bottle and will produce enough carbon dioxide, now confined in the bottle by the wired cork, to give the wine its ultimate sparkle.

This bottled wine now goes for its long rest in the cool, damp cellars where it will remain quietly for at least two or three years. It is said that there are 100 miles of these cellars holding millions of bottles of Champagne.[1] This represents a considerable tie-up of capital and accounts in part for the cost of the bottle you buy in the shop.[2]

During this long rest in the cellars the slow fermentation, induced by the dose of sugar at bottling time, will produce sediment that must be eliminated if the wine is to be perfectly clear—which it must be. The bottles have been lying flat and this sediment has collected on the lower side of the bottle. The bottles are now moved to another part of the cellars and placed neck downward at an angle of 60 degrees in 'pulpits'. In this position every one of millions of bottles is given a quick twist every day for several weeks to dislodge the sediment from the side of the bottle and cause it to settle just behind the cork. This operation is called *rémuage* (shaking). A man deft at this job will twist some 30,000 bottles a day.

At the end of this three months' shaking a skilled worker, called a *dégorgeur* (disgorger), removes the wire, withdraws the cork and the pressure of the gas blows out

[1] In July 1964 there were 230 million.
[2] A larger item is the high tax imposed on sparkling wines, be they good or bad.

Dégorgeur. *Photo courtesy of Lanson père et fils.*

the wad of sediment. It is hard to believe, but he does this with very little loss of wine. He claps on a temporary cap and passes the bottle to another man at his side who will give the wine its final dose of sugar, called the Liqueur d'Expédition (shipment liquor). At this point the wine is completely dry or 'natural'. After its long fermentation no sugar remains. It is called *vin brut* by the cellar men but if any of it is bottled without the dose of sugar it will be labelled *Nature*. The dosage varies according to the degree of dryness or sweetness wanted to meet the requirements of the maker's clientele.

*Champagne Vintages*

Champagne is always a blend of wine and often the blend will contain some of the wine of previous years. A vintage Champagne will be essentially a blend of wines of the year in which the grapes were grown. If the year were an exceptionally good one, 'vintage' may well be superior in some respects to non-vintage. In fact Champagne *should* be bottled as vintage only in good years. But some consumers are snobbish about vintage, believing non-vintage to be second-rate and they couldn't think of offering it to their guests. In private, few would be able to tell the difference. If you buy the non-vintage of any top grade House you will always enjoy the same quality—and often at less cost. Non-vintage is not so labelled; absence of the year on the neck label indicates non-vintage.

If you lean to vintage don't go too far back. Champagne doesn't live long as do many of the still wines— ten years is about the limit. It is already three years old when it goes to market. As to types of Champagne, i.e. nature, brut, sec (dry), Goût Americain, etc., my preference is for nature or brut produced by an old and reputable House.

Sparkling white wines that look like Champagne and have similar bubbles are made in many countries. In Germany it is called *Sekt*, in Italy *Spumante*, in Spain Spanish Champagne.[1] None of these imitations equals in character and quality the product of a reputable French House.

But a number of wine makers in this country produce

[1] As the result of a legal battle in England a few years ago, the sparkling wine of Spain cannot be labelled 'champagne' if shipped to England.

Visitors being conducted through the extensive cellars
of Mercier & Co., Rheims.
*Photo courtesy of Mercier & Co.*

really excellent 'champagne'. One that we like at our house is Great Western, made by Pleasant Valley Wine Company in the Finger Lakes district at Hammondsport, New York. This wine is made from native varieties of grape and is fermented in bottle in precisely the same way as in France.

In California are a dozen or more wineries that produce champagne. Some of these are rarely available in the East. We often drink a bottle of Almaden. This is bottled-fermented and comes as close to French methods as any.

71

# The Wines of Germany

As has been said earlier, the ratio of fine wines to total production is higher in Germany than in France. But when you remember that France's production is at least ten times Germany's, the statistic shows only that German wine growers are passionately devoted to the making of fine wines and highly skilled in the art.

Germany grows both red and white wines but one can ignore the reds; only two or three are worthy of notice. None has either the quality or the distinction of the better red wines of France. When speaking of German wines it is white wines one has in mind and some of these are amongst the finest in the world.

The wine-growing region in Germany, as will be seen on the map, is in the south-west in the valleys of the Rhine and Moselle rivers. No other part of the country is suitable for wine grapes—too far north. Wine districts are delimited, more or less as in France, their boundaries being those of administrative areas or of natural geographical divisions. These are Mosel-Saar-Ruwer, usually referred to as Moselle (the Saar and the Ruwer are small tributaries), Rheingau, Rheinhesse, Rheinpfalz, and two minor districts—Nahe (nah), a river valley lying between Rheinhesse and the Moselle, and Franconia (*Franken* in German) on the river Main (mine) some distance east of the Rhine.

The Moselle rises in France and flows through Germany from the French border to Coblenz where it joins the Rhine. In Germany it is spelled Mosel, pro-

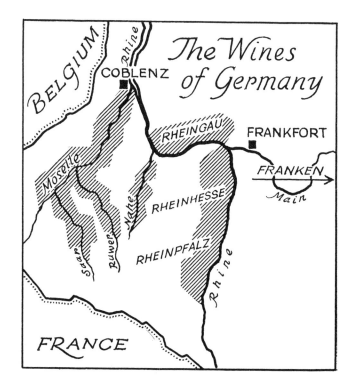

nounced Moz'l. It is a river of sharp and frequent bends,
flowing in a deep valley with terraced vineyards on both
sides. From these terraces come many fine wines, the
yield of back-breaking toil and the meticulous care and
skill characteristic of the German people. They produce
delightful, delicate wines, hardly equalled in these
respects by any others.

I used to travel frequently to Frankfort and at the
renowned Frankfurter Hof I never failed to drink a half
bottle of 'Moz'l' with my lunch. It is perfectly delightful.

73

And here is the proper place to mention some of the better vineyard properties in the valley.

One of the best known, partly due to its curious name, is Berncasteler *Doktor*—often spelled with 'c' instead of 'k'). Berncastel is a township in the Moselle district and the 'er' suffix (universally used in German wine nomenclature) means simply *of*, i.e. *of* Berncastel. Doktor is the name of a vineyard owned many years ago by a Dr Thanisch. Parts of it are still the property of the family. Another Moselle, also popular, due to its attractive name, is Piesporter *Goldtröpfchen*—'little drops of gold'—from the township of Piesport.

Other excellent Moselles which you will do well to remember when you want to buy a fine one are Graacher *Himmelreich*, Trittenheimer *Laurentiusberg*, Wehlener *Sonnenuhr* (Sundial), Zeltinger *Rotlay*, Piesporter *Lay*, Erdener *Treppchen* (little steps or stairs), probably so called due to its steep-terraced vineyards. There are many others of equally high repute—trust the label, a reliable importer and an honest wine merchant —there is no 'appellation contrôlée' in Germany.

At the very top of the Moselles and ranking with the finest wines of Germany is *Scharzhofberg* in the township of Wiltingen on the Saar river. Frank Schoonmaker in his *Encyclopedia of Wine*[1] praises it in these words: 'Few wine names and few wine labels are accorded such unhesitating respect by wine lovers in all countries.' The name stands on its own—no need to mention the township. Find a bottle of it to give to your wife on your next wedding anniversary.

At lower prices than the wines with vineyard names

[1] Hastings House, 1964.

74

A typical German label—see guide on page 85.

are those with communal, or township names—plain Berncasteler, for example, usually blends of wine from two or more vineyards in the township. Blends of Moselle which will consist of wines from anywhere in the district will be a bit cheaper still. *Moselblümchen*— 'little flowers of the Moselle'—is a name used by a number of shippers. If you buy one of these, have a care for the name of a reliable shipper and importer. Without infringing any regulation Moselblümchen may be a catch-all of pretty ordinary wines. If the price is much less than a plain Bernkastler (or a wine of any other township), you'd better reject it. On the other hand it may be quite pleasant—it depends on who bottled it.

The Moselles are light wines, alcohol—from 8 to 10 per cent, and are delightful as beverage wines to be drunk by themselves as well as with the appropriate food.

## RHEINGAU

To explain why this small district produces more fine wines than any other in Germany it is necessary to introduce a bit of geography. From its source in Switzerland the Rhine flows in a northerly direction to Holland and the North Sea except for a sharp detour about midway of its course. Here it meets the barrier of the Taunus Hills and bends to a west-south-west direction. After twenty miles it resumes its northerly course just beyond the historic town of Bingen. Along this stretch of the broad river the vineyards on its right bank face the sun and, as if that were not enough, the high and heavily wooded hills shield them from the cold north winds. Apart from the fact that the Rheingau is pretty far north for wine, no more favoured position exists anywhere. Here are grown, on no more than 5,000 acres of terraced hillsides, the finest wines of Germany and certainly some of the finest white wines of the whole world. The district is called Rheingau—Rhine County.

In this small area—a fourth the size of the Moselle region—are townships and villages whose wines have made themselves famous throughout the world where fine wines are known and appreciated. Here are the names of some of these towns which, with the 'er' suffix, will be found on bottle labels; Rüdesheim, Johannisberg, Hattenheim, Rauenthal, Erbach, Eltville, Hochheim. Other famous names, not of towns or villages, but of vineyard properties, are *Steinberg* in the township of Hattenheim, *Schloss Vollrads* in the township of Winkel, and *Schloss Johannisberg*, the most renowned of all, in the township of Johannisberg.

1962er Rotlack

Schloss Johannisberger.

Original Abfüllung der
Fürst von Metternichschen
Domäne.
Rheingau

Rhine Wine
Product of Germany

Wappen der Fürsten
von Metternich - Winneburg

Contents: 1 Pint 8 Fl. Oz. - Alcohol 11 % by Volume

## RHEINHESSE

Across the river south of the Rheingau is the district of
Rheinhesse. Here the production is far greater than in
the Rheingau—30,000 acres of vines compared with
Rheingau's 5,000—and the wines are by no means up to
the Rheingau level of quality. How could they be with
an annual yield of some 14 million gallons? For the
most part the wines of the Rheinhesse are quite ordinary.
Much of the lower grade wine goes to market as Liebfraumilch. But there are eight or ten townships near the
river which produce good, and some really fine, wines.
Three of these that you can usefully and easily remember
are Nierstein, Nackenheim and Oppenheim.

For some reason the wines of Nierstein seem to enjoy
a greater popularity in this country than the others. You
will find Niersteiners in almost every wine shop that
carries a selection of Rhine wines. The cheapest will be
labelled simply Niersteiner and, though often quite

77

pleasant, will have no distinction. What you should look for is a Niersteiner with a vineyard name. Among the better ones are Niersteiner *Rehbach*, Niersteiner *Hipping*, Niersteiner *Auflangen*—there are at least a dozen. Study the label and trust an honest wine merchant.

When you are looking for one of these you are almost sure to come across a Niersteiner *Domtal*. Though Domtal *sounds* like a vineyard name, it is nothing of the sort. The grower or shipper who puts it on a bottle label probably hopes you will think it is. Dom means cathedral and tal means valley, so Domtal is simply cathedral valley—a wine without a birth certificate. The name can now be applied legally to any wine grown in the township of Nierstein. This is one of the rare (and regrettable) perversions of the German wine law. A wine so ticketed will probably not be as good as a plain unembellished Niersteiner. One can imagine the perpetrator of this mild deception saying to himself on tasting one of his wines preparatory to bottling: 'It's not up to much; call it Domtal, price it a bit higher and we shall get rid of it.' I believe there was once a vineyard called Domtal but it has long since lost its exclusivity.

And while on the subject of wine-law quirks, I may as well warn you of *Dorf*. In German Dorf is the word for village. It, too, may be taken to be the name of a vineyard. As it is used on a German wine label it precedes the name of the district or village—usually one of renown. I don't know of a 'Dorf Niersteiner' but there is a Dorf Johannisberger. This, of course, can be any wine from the township of Johannisberg—a name of magical value in German wine nomenclature due to the fame of Schloss Johannisberg.[1] As to the other eight or ten townships in Rheinhesse producing fine wines—Nackenheim and Oppenheim, for example—their wines will compare favourably with those of Nierstein. You will find it interesting to try some of them if you happen to find them. None will be of the superior quality of the wines of the Rheingau.

RHEINPFALZ, or PALATINATE

This is ancient wine country—the name itself comes from Rome. Pfalz is German for Palatinate and our word *palace* is derived from it. Latin scholars will remember that Palatine was one of the seven hills of Rome where the luxury-loving Roman emperors built their palaces.

The district lies directly south of Rheinhesse, still on the left bank of the Rhine. It is the largest in Germany, yielding some 15 million gallons of wine a year. A good deal of ordinary red wine is grown but, as elsewhere, white wine predominates by a wide margin. Much of the terrain is flat and fertile, unsuitable for the production of fine wine. Little of this wine is bottled, much less exported. This is *Tischwein* (table wine), drawn from the cask in hundreds of *weinstuben* throughout the country.

But in a few townships some excellent wine is grown. Chief among them are Forst, Deidesheim, Rupertsberg and Wachenheim. Leading vineyards, whose names you will find on bottle labels and wine lists, are: in *Forst*—

[1] As to Dorf, it resembles *Beaujolais Villages* but with the important difference that Beaujolais Villages is an officially recognized 'Appellation' in France and its use on a bottle label is under the strict control of the Institut National des Appellations d'Origine.

Jesuitengarten, Kirchenstück, Ungeheuer and Elster; in *Deidesheim*—Kieselberg, Langenmorgen, Herrgott-sacker; in *Rupertsberg*—Mandelacker, Hofstück, Hoheburg, and Reiterpfad; in *Wachenheim*—Goldbachel, Gerumpel, Böhlig and Schenkenbohl. Look for these names when you want the very best. Most of the limited number of fine wines are estate-bottled—*original abfüllung*—and the critical facts about them will appear on the label. Some of these will be amongst the most costly German wines.

## NAHE

This district lying west of Rheinhesse gets its name from the small river Nahe (nah), which flows in a north-easterly direction to join the Rhine at Bingen. There are some 4,000 acres of vines, yielding two million gallons of wine a year.

Nahe wines are similar to the Niersteiners but with something of the liveliness of the Moselles. If you come across a Nahe wine it may be a bit lower in price than a comparable Moselle as it is less well known in this country. The best known vineyard is called *Schloss Böckelheim* and there are many others.

## FRANCONIA, or FRANKEN

This is a minor, but nonetheless important wine district. It is in north-western Bavaria, some 70 miles east of the Rhine. It is thus quite detached from Rhine wine country, similar in this respect to Chablis in relation to Burgundy. The district lies along the river Main (pronounced *mine*) and at this part of its winding course it flows between vine-clad hills that rise from both its

1959
Würzburger Jesuitenstein
SCHEU-RIESLING
Arthur Hallgarten G.m.b.H.
Oestrich-Winkel (Rheingau)
Produce of Germany
FRANKEN

banks. At the centre of the district, and of the wine industry, is the ancient town of Würzburg.

Only white wine is grown and it has a distinctive character not easy to define. Perhaps the professional tasters have called it 'steely' or 'flinty'. It is, almost without exception, very dry and its colour the palest amber. It is popularly known as Steinwein and is bottled in squat, green flagons called Bocksbeutel (bawks-boy-'tl).

Steinwein is a regional designation such as Moselle or Burgundy but it is inappropriate and, in a strict sense, inaccurate. In Germany the generic term is *Frankenwein*. What can be correctly called Steinwein—or more specifically Würzburger Stein—is the wine of a vineyard called *Stein* on the rocky slopes of the Steinberg hills directly south of the town.

There are several other vineyards in Würzburg and you will find their wines under their vineyard names.

They will not be labelled 'Steinwein' but that is what to ask for at your wine merchant's. You can then pursue the subject and find out what Franconian wines he has in stock. One that I find agreeable is Würzberger *Jesuitenstein*. Other vineyard towns in the district are: Echerndorf, Rödelsee, Randsacker and Iphofen. Though these are shipped as Steinwein, this is as wide of the mark as it would be to call all Bordeaux wines Saint Emilion. Good Franconian wines cost from $3 to $4 in most New York shops.

## FANTASIE NAMEN

In a class quite apart from wines with place names are those with what the Germans call *fantasie namen*—fanciful names. They have great commercial value but that is about all they are worth. Unlike the honest place names already described, they give no information on the origin of the wine in the bottle and are likely to be misleading to anyone not familiar with this peculiarity of German nomenclature.

The most widely known fanciful name is *Liebfraumilch*. It arose presumably from the name of a church in the old city of Worms, called Liebfrauenkirche, the Church of Our Lady.

It is surrounded by a 25-acre vineyard—once an appendage of the church. Its wine was properly called *Liebfrauenstiftswein*, and is so marketed today, but many years ago someone had the idea to christen it Liebfraumilch—literally Milk of the Blessed Mother. It is perhaps unlikely that the inventor of the name had any inkling of its extraordinary sales value.

The name is unregistered and unprotected—any

wine maker or shipper can apply it to any German wine or blend of wines of whatever origin. Many of the low-grade wines of the Rheinhesse are successfully marketed under this alluring label. When you buy one of these you will be paying tribute to the famous name at a sacrifice to the worth of the wine in the bottle. A plain Niersteiner may well be the better value.

But there are exceptions. The name has such great selling power that a number of reputable and old-established shippers use it, in spite of its general derogatory connotation. Some of these Houses have added their own registered trade name to distinguish *their* Liebfraumilch from dozens of others of doubtful merit. But even these high grade shippers are forbidden by law to include in their label any words or pictures which might be taken to indicate a source of origin of the wine.

Another fancy name is *Zeller Schwarze Katz*—the Black Cat of Zell. This, in a rather harmless way, is misleading because Schwarze Katz, following the place name of Zell, sounds unmistakably like a vineyard name. It isn't. It is a name 'dreamed up', someone has said, by an enterprising mayor of Zell. However far this may be from truth, the inventor of the Black Cat did great service to the little vineyard township.

Zell is situated in the lower Moselle valley, too far down the river for the growing of fine wines and far too small to yield the large quantity of Zeller Schwarze Katz marketed so successfully in this and other English-speaking countries. The wine is a blend of quite ordinary Moselles and shippers can buy them where they will. There is always a picture on the label of the

Ancient Liebfrauenkirche surrounded by its vineyards.
*Photo courtesy of German Tourist Office, London.*

scrappy looking feline and often a back label tells
you an intriguing story of his exploits in an ancient
wine cellar.

*Kröver Nacktarsch* is still another fancy name as meaningless as Zeller Schwarze Katz. It emanates from the
township of Kröv, a bit up river from Zell. Instead of
the black cat on the label there is a picture of a small
boy with his pants down being spanked on his bare
bottom. Nacktarsch apparently means *naked behind.*
This somewhat naïve presentation has sold a lot of
wine. It is a blend of ordinary Moselles, probably un-
able to merit bottling on their own.

84

The main thing to remember about these three fancy names is that they may conceal a low quality of the wine in the bottle. Better value will be had from ordinary wines with simple district names.

## GERMAN WINE VINTAGES

Most labels give the vintage of the wine in the bottle. Since German wine-growing districts are close to the northern limit of the wine belt, the quality of the wine is more apt to vary from year to year. Late frost in the spring, early frost in the fall, too much rain, not enough rain and other varying weather factors determine the quality of the wine. Vintages vary more than they do in France and other countries to the south. Recent good vintages in general—though they vary from one district to another—have been 1961, 1962, 1964 and 1966.

## GUIDE TO GERMAN WINE LABELS

Many of these terms will be found on labels reproduced in the text. Here is a quick run-down on their meaning:

*Abzug:* to draw off from.

*Abfüllung:* bottling, e.g. Kellerabfüllung—bottled in the cellar.

*Auslese:* selected bunches of grapes set aside for special pressing.

*Beerenauslese:* selected berries (grapes), snipped from bunches with long thin scissors.

*Cresenz:* growth, i.e. vineyard or part of.

*Gewächs:* growth, i.e. vineyard or part of.

*Kabinett* (or Cabinet)*:* a term used to designate an extra special wine.

*Keller:* wine cellar.

*Kellerei:* wine cellars—often wine house or blending and bottling plant.

*Kellerabfüllung:* bottled in the cellar—any cellar.

*Naturwein* (or naturrein, natur, rein)*:* indicates wine fermented without the addition of sugar.

85

*Originalabfüllung:* bottled in the grower's own cellar—a positive guarantee of authenticity.

*Original Kellerabfüllung:* bottled in the grower's own cellar—a positive guarantee of authenticity.

*Original Kellerabzug:* bottled in the grower's own cellar—a positive guarantee of authenticity.

*Sonderabfüllung:* sonder means special but what 'special' means is open to question.

*Spätlese:* late harvested, i.e. made from grapes left on the vines beyond the official date for the termination of the harvest—in general a sweeter, fuller-bodied wine and more costly.

*Trockenbeerenauslese:* selected individual grapes that have been left on the vine until much of the water in the juice has been absorbed by the *Edelfäule* (the 'pourriture noble' of France) similar to the practice in the Sauternes district. Often fetches an astronomical price.

*Wachstum:* literally 'growth', i.e. the name of a vineyard, or part of, followed by the name of the owner.

*Weingut:* winery—definitely not a Growth, and usually no indication of authenticity.

In all of the foregoing the important word is *Original*. When this word is used it is a guarantee of the accuracy of all the information on the label. If it is absent most of the other information is without much significance.

# The Wines of Italy

Italy is the second largest wine producer in the world[1]—
a billion and a half gallons a year—and the Italians
themselves drink most of it. Only about 3 per cent of
this vast quantity is exported and perhaps half of what
comes to this country is drunk by Italo-Americans,
loyal to the homeland of their ancestors. Considerably
smaller in total area than the State of California, Italy
produces nearly ten times as much wine.

There are thousands of small vineyards whose wine is
sold only locally and perhaps an equal number of back-
yard plots whose home-made product is consumed by
their owners and next-door neighbours. On the other
hand there are many large vineyard properties and co-
operatives which produce excellent wines. But no
Italian wine (or any other for that matter) ranks in
quality with the superior wines of France and Germany.

No uniform system of nomenclature exists with
respect to Italian wines. A wine takes the name of the
place where it is grown or the name of the variety of
grape from which it is made. So far as I know there is
no definable reason for the choice between the two.
Barolo is a place name, that of a town in the centre of a
small district in the Piedmont, near Italy's northern
border with France.

Near Barolo is the town of Barbaresco, and its wine is
so called, but in the same district are wines called
Barbera and Grignolino, which are grape varieties.

[1] France and Italy are neck and neck as to volume of production.

VECCHIO VINO
di
BARBARESCO
ANTICO PODERE CONTI della CREMOSINA

Dr. Arturo Bersano-Nizza Monferrato (Asti · Italia)

Chianti, the Italian wine best known outside Italy, gets its name not from a town or a grape but from a low range of mountains in the province of Tuscany. All this appears to be without rhyme or reason; it's rather confusing and doesn't really matter much.

There are no laws or regulations in Italy with respect to labelling that are anything like the French 'Appellation Contrôlée' or the meticulous system of designation and control operative in Germany. The average Italian, like the Spaniard, is little interested in such details. He learned as a child that red wine is as indispensable as spaghetti, and he isn't too fussy about it.

Around 1930 an effort was made to delimit and to identify many wine districts and by official action limit the use of the names of wines to their respective districts. High hopes were expressed that this would bring order to the Italian wine industry but these were not to be realized.

Chianti is a good example. The wine is grown in a relatively small area between Siena and Florence in the province of Tuscany. An official regulation, promulgated in 1932, aimed to put an end to the indiscriminate and misleading use of the designation of a wine as Chianti. It set limits to the traditional, or 'classic', Chianti district and authorized growers in the delimited area to ticket their wine 'Chianti Classico'. To give added weight to the provisions of the regulation a symbol was devised—a picture of a cock, which growers within the area could affix to the bottle seal. For a time these indicators were a guarantee of genuine Chianti— but not for long, for the simple reason that the regulation did not prohibit the use of the words 'Chianti Classico' by growers *outside* the district. So these words on the neck label and the cock on the bottle cap have become largely meaningless.[1]

Many wines produced in vineyards contiguous to the 'classical' area are as good or better than many ticketed 'classico'. Some famous growers ignored or have abandoned the words all together, preferring to give their wine their own name, usually coupled with the name of the town or village from which it came. These superior Chiantis usually come in straight-sided Bordeaux-type bottles, not in the familiar straw-covered flask.

The leading wine district of Italy, both as to volume of production and the quality of its wines, is in the

[1] A new effort has been under way for the past two years to provide Italian wine growers with government backing as to the Appellation of origin of their wines. It is hoped that this may become effective soon. Makers will be able, if they comply with the strict regulations, to add to their label the words Denominazione di Origin Controllata e Garantiti— Appellation of Origin Controlled and Guaranteed. Any wine producer may apply for the privilege but the requirements are stiff. Many have already applied.

Piedmont (Piemonte) whose commercial centre is Turin, the Fiat city. The best Piedmont wine, and one widely regarded as the best red wine of Italy, is Barolo. This is a lusty wine that needs considerable age to bring it to perfection. Normally it is kept in casks for several years but, even so, it throws a heavy deposit in bottle and should be decanted when served. It is made from the Nebbiolo grape, the variety most widely cultivated in the Piedmont. Other good wines from the district, lighter than Barolo, are Barbaresco, Grignolino and Barbera. Asti Spumante, the Italian 'champagne', a rather sweet sparkling wine, comes from the town of Asti, not far from Turin.

East of the Piedmont is the province of Venetia and here there are two well-known red wines—Bardolino, a town, and Valpolicella, a valley. Both are lighter in body and colour than the red Piedmont wines. Also from this district comes an excellent pale green, dry white wine called Soave, from the town of that name. To the north-east, reaching to the border of Austria, is the Italian Tyrol where a great variety of both red and white wine is grown. The district is called Trentino Alto Adige—Adige being a river. This area was long under Austrian domination and many of its wines retain German names. Viticulture and wine making are in an advanced stage of development and we may expect some excellent wines when they reach these shores. They are not widely imported at present.

Back now to the Mediterranean coast and southward toward Rome where we meet with Orvieto, an excellent white wine that reminds one of a dry graves from Bordeaux. On toward Naples we come to Lacrima Christi, a delicate, sweet white wine grown on the lower slopes of Mount Vesuvius. This wine, like the Liebfraumilch of Germany, owes much of its popularity abroad to its lovely name, meaning Tears of Christ.

Italian wines generally cost less in the United States than comparable French wines. They are available everywhere; try them. Their food affinities are similar to those of French wines but, somehow or other, they seem to go particularly well with spaghetti and other Italian pastas. This may be nothing more than an association of ideas but if it contributes to the full enjoyment of these dishes, that's a good enough reason for uniting them.

# The Wines of Spain and Portugal

The famous wine of Spain is Sherry, and of Portugal, Port. Both of these wines, known for centuries around the world, are described at length in a chapter of their own. The volume produced is not more than about two per cent of each country's total production.

What we are concerned with here are table wines and both countries produce them in vast quantities. Spain is, in fact, the world's third largest producer and in some years the largest exporter. If bad weather or some other calamity cuts the yield of France's vineyards, Spain comes to her rescue. Portugal produces nearly four times as much table wine as the United States and *per capita* consumption is 25 gallons a year compared with less than half a gallon in this country. In recent years, shipments to the United States have been on the increase and table wines from Spain are to be had at prices often considerably lower, east of the Mississippi at any rate, than comparable 'standard' wines of California. Last year in Connecticut a good Spanish wine for our everyday drinking could be had for $1.25 a bottle.

The best Spanish table wines come from the Rioja (ree-oh-ha), a district in the valley of the Ebro river not far from the French border at Biarritz-San Sebastian. Many of the wines grown here are excellent, particularly the reds. When you go to buy them look for the word Rioja on the label and for a stamp-like identification mark. You will see it on the label reproduced here.

Around the border are the words CONSEJO REGULADOR DENOMINACION ORIGEN—Council for the Regulation of Names of Origin. This is a reliable guarantee of a genuine Rioja wine and an indication of good quality. The privilege of using the mark is granted by the Spanish Government only to highly reputable producers and shippers.

Most of the Spanish table wines imported into this country are standard blends, designated as Claret or Burgundy for the red wines and Chablis for the white. Few have vineyard names but here are two that you may come across: Villa Zaco and Castel Pomal. These usually are priced a bit higher than the blends. Haro and Logroño are townships in the Rioja district. Vintage (in Spanish *Cosecha*) is often stated on labels but not too much reliance can be placed on it. In any case it doesn't matter much.

## PORTUGAL

The best table wine of Portugal comes from a district

called *Dāo* which lies about half-way between Lisbon and Oporto. Others that we may expect to find in many wine shops are the white wines of the north called *Vinho Verde*, literally green wines, which merely means that they are to be drunk when quite young, and *Colares*, grown not far from Lisbon. The Portuguese wines most popular in the United States at present are two brands of rosé—Mateus and Lancers—both extensively advertised. Compare these with the rosés of France and California and see what you think of them.

# The Wines of the United States

The United States produces well over 200 million gallons of wine a year. This is a lot of wine and the basis of a substantial industry, but France, smaller than Texas, produces seven times as much. And if we consider table wines alone—those with which this guide is chiefly concerned—the ratio is about 20 to 1.

The American wine industry differs radically from that of any wine country in Europe. In France and Germany alone there are close on a half million individual vineyard owners; in the United States there are perhaps 15,000. Here wine is 'big business'; in Europe it is a vast collection of small growers and a large share of these make their own wine. This is why there are so many thousands of different European wines, each with its own name. This, along with widely differing soils and climates, accounts for the infinite variety in the wines of the Old World and the fascinating 'romance' of wine.[1]

American wines have suffered as a result of being called by the age-old place names of Europe. This inevitably invited comparison and a verdict of inferiority for the American. If these wines had been given names of their own, following the interlude of prohibition when the opportunity was wide open, they sooner would have taken their rightful place among the wines

[1] In California five or six companies make about 70 per cent of all wine produced. New York State's 12 million gallons a year is made chiefly by four big companies.

of the world. Frank Schoonmaker and Tom Marvel, who, together, wrote two important books on wine[1] in this period (1934 and 1941), made a valiant fight for this reform but their efforts were doomed to failure. The hungry wine makers took the easy route to profits and offered to a largely unsuspecting public the wine labels they remembered. What was in the bottle mattered little.

I have said that the effort was doomed to failure— and so it was at the time but in the past decade it has borne fruit with gratifying results. Nearly all of the better California and New York State wines now have varietal names—and district names to go with them are not uncommon. These names have begun to have real significance to wine drinkers in this country.

A useful device of American wine-makers is the back label which gives additional information on the wine in the bottle. Some of these contain a bit of sales talk as well but this is easily spotted and can be excused. Names apart, your best guide to the quality of the wine in the bottle is the name of a reliable and conscientious wine maker.

Much good wine is made in the United States but if we are to appreciate its merits we must stop comparing it with the wines of France and Germany.[2] The plain fact is that no American wine equals in quality the

[1] *The Complete Wine Book*, Simon & Schuster, New York, 1934—now out of print and fetching a high price. *American Wines*, Duell, Sloan & Pearce, 1941.

[2] Dr Maynard A. Amerine, Professor of Oenology (science of wine) at the University of California, has said (as quoted in the *New York Times* of May 30, 1965): 'I do not think the wines are or should be comparable.' He added, 'It is no secret that California Claret, Burgundy, and Chianti are not distinguishable types of wine. Such labels mean nothing.'

finer wines of these two countries. Let this be your starting point if you are to get acquainted with the good wines of the United States. Perhaps the best way to do this is to stop drinking French, German and other European wines for a month or two and drink only American wines. Forget Claret, Burgundy, Chablis, Sauternes and Rhine wine and judge American wines purely on their merits. If you do this you very likely will find a number of them that you like.

Most of the larger and better-known makers of table wines produce, in addition to their varietal wines, 'standard' types, marketed usually under regional names of foreign origin such as Bordeaux, i.e. Claret, Burgundy, Chablis, Rhine and 'Sauterne'. These wines are blends, made up of two or more varieties of grape and often of two or three wines of previous years. The aim of the wine maker is to maintain, year after year, a standard type.

These wines are grown in the company's own vineyards, supplemented normally by other wines bought from small growers in the district. Frequently, too, the ripe grapes are bought from these growers and taken to the company's winery where they are crushed and fermented. Let me hasten to say that there is nothing incorrect or unethical in this procedure; in fact wine thus produced has the advantage of being always much the same, and it costs you less. Hundreds of highly reputable growers and shippers of France, Germany, Spain and Italy produce 'standard' wines in this manner. The best way to find out which standard wines you like is to try them one after another. When you have found what you like you can stick to it. For variety, drink other 'standard' wines of the same general type made by different makers.

## CALIFORNIA WINES

The best California table wines are grown in the valleys and on the hillsides around or near San Francisco Bay, an area best designated as the North Coast Counties. Here varieties of the European grape, the *Vitis vinifera*, were first planted well over 100 years ago. Both soil and climate in this area are propitious—relatively cool summers, a mild winter, sufficient sunshine and moisture, soil not too rich and sufficiently varied to yield good, sound wine and, in the better grades, fine wines of individual character.

Until comparatively recently the growing of fine table wines was almost entirely confined to the Bay counties but one of them, Santa Clara, has now been virtually eliminated due to the encroachment of industrial and urban development. Two leading wine growers, sensing this menace, have set out thousands of acres of vines some hundred miles to the south in San Benito and Monterey counties.

Before doing so exhaustive research was undertaken in these new areas and, surprisingly, it was found that both soil and climate were wholly appropriate for fine-wine cultivation. So San Benito and Monterey counties must now be classed along with the North Coast group, and these names may begin soon to make their appearance on bottle labels. Another quality producer, Wente Brothers, of the Livermore valley, have felt the ill wind of urbanization and they, too, have planted some 800 acres in the district.

*Beaulieu Vineyard*

ESTATE BOTTLED

## CHATEAU BEAULIEU®
NAPA VALLEY MEDIUM SWEET
### SAUVIGNON BLANC

PRODUCED & BOTTLED BY BEAULIEU VINEYARD
AT RUTHERFORD, NAPA COUNTY, CALIFORNIA
ALCOHOL 11% BY VOLUME

This BV label leaves nothing to be desired. It gives you the name of the producer, Beaulieu Vineyard; the name of the grape the wine is made from, Sauvignon Blanc; the place where the grapes were grown, Napa Valley; and a guide to the wine's principal taste characteristic, medium sweet. If a district name is added to the varietal name 75 per cent of the wine must come from grapes grown in the district named.

By far the best of California wines are the *varietals*—wines made from the juice of one grape—or essentially from one. California regulations require that any wine ticketed as a varietal, e.g. Pinot Noir, Cabernet Sauvignon, Chardonnay, must be made from a minimum of 51 per cent of the juice of the named grape. Many varietals contain 100 per cent, many come pretty close to it. If the district is stated on the label, 75 per cent of the grapes used in the wine must come from the district named. The leading varietals are the following:

99

*Vineyards Established 1852*

## ALMADÉN
*California Mountain*
### PINOT NOIR

A distinguished, authentic Pinot Noir, velvety and fine,
made entirely from grapes of this illustrious Burgundian variety,
grown in Mountain Vineyards at Paicines, California

PRODUCED AND BOTTLED BY
Almadén Vineyards, Los Gatos, California
Alcohol 12½% by volume

CABERNET SAUVIGNON (cab-er-nay so-vee-nyon)

This is the outstanding red wine grape of the Bordeaux region in France. The great red wines of the Médoc are made largely from it. It is a 'noble' grape; without doubt one of the finest red wine grapes of the world. When you have become familiar with wine made from it in California you should have no difficulty in recognizing it. The wine will not have the *finesse* of the great wines of Bordeaux but it will be one of the two best red wines grown in the United States.

PINOT NOIR (pee-no-nwahr)

I have just said that the Cabernet Sauvignon is one of the world's superior red wine grapes. The Pinot Noir is the other one. All the great red Burgundies of the Côte d'Or in France are made from it and it is the principal constituent of French champagnes. A number of growers in the north coast counties cultivate the Pinot Noir and produce from it excellent red wines. Even more justifiably than the Cabernet Sauvignon, wine from the Pinot Noir cannot be low in price. Its yield per acre is considerably less and its cultivation is difficult.

CHARDONNAY or PINOT CHARDONNAY (shar-don-nay)
This is the great white wine grape of Burgundy in France, the superb variety that yields Montrachet—the best white wine of the Côte d'Or and perhaps the finest white wine in the whole world. The Chardonnay is used extensively in champagne. Like many others, the Chardonnay in California does not reach the supreme quality of its French counterpart but it is the source of possibly the best white wine made in the United States. This grape is used also in most of the better grades of California champagne.

WHITE RIESLING or JOHANNISBERG RIESLING (reese-ling)
The Riesling is the supreme grape of the white wines of the Moselle and Rhine in Germany. A good deal of juggling with this famous name has gone on in California. The true Riesling is called either White Riesling or Johannisberg Riesling to distinguish it from many inferior kinds using the name Riesling.

SAUVIGNON BLANC (so-vee-nyon)
This is one of the finer white wine grapes of the world, grown extensively in the Graves and Sauternes dis-

tricts of Bordeaux. In the north coast counties, it yields a fine, full-bodied wine similar to a dry Graves.

## SEMILLON (sem-me-yon)

Another of the white wine grapes of France, somewhat similar to the Sauvignon Blanc. In the making of the great French Sauternes the two varieties are often fermented together—one complementing the other. In California the Semillon by itself renders a smooth white wine—rather on the dry side like a first grade Graves.

Other varietal wines are made from *Zinfandel*, a red wine grape of vague European origin, now grown widely in California but apparently nowhere else. *Sylvaner* and *Traminer* (tra-mee-ner), Alsatian varieties of white grapes, *Grenache* (gren-ash), largely used in making vin rosé; *Gamay* (gam-may), the principal red wine grape of the Beaujolais district in France; *Chenin Blanc* (shay-nan-blawn), the white grape of the Loire; *Barbera* and *Grignolino* (green-yo-leen-o), red wine grapes of Italy— and many others, some good and some not so good.

## CALIFORNIA CHAMPAGNE

Champagne is made by a number of wineries in the north coast counties and much of it is excellent. The process is the same as the French one and the same grape varieties are used. The only way for you to find out which brands you like best is to try them one after another. One that we drink much of the time and with satisfaction is Almaden's, which compares favourably with Great Western, one of the better champagnes of

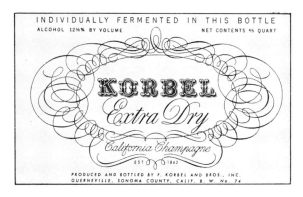

INDIVIDUALLY FERMENTED IN THIS BOTTLE
ALCOHOL 12½% BY VOLUME                    NET CONTENTS ⅘ QUART

KORBEL

*Extra Dry*

*California Champagne*

EST 1862

PRODUCED AND BOTTLED BY F. KORBEL AND BROS., INC.
GUERNEVILLE, SONOMA COUNTY, CALIF. B. W. No. 74

New York State. Here are the names of a half dozen good brands: Almaden, Beaulieu, Korbel, Hans Kornell, Paul Masson and Weibel.

## CALIFORNIA SHERRY

Some good sherry is made by leading wineries of the north coast counties. The ideal grape is the Palomino, grown in the hot country of the central valley. This is the grape responsible for all of the fine Spanish sherries. As will be seen in the chapter on Sherry, it is not only the grape that is important but the soil of the district; and nothing like it exists in California. However, a number of producers in California have succeeded in making pretty good sherry.

A few of these age their sherry in soleras, others 'bake' the wine in huge vats where it is held at a temperature of around 120 degrees for six months or more, aimed to bring about, through oxidation, the characteristic sherry flavour. This baking process is a modernized adaptation of the system used in conditioning Madeira and Marsala. This method gets the wine to the consumer quicker and costs less than the slower working solera. My preference is for the solera system described in detail in the chapter on Sherry and at our house we often serve Almaden's *Cocktail Sherry*. It suits us far better than any of the non-Spanish sherries that we occasionally drank last winter in London. In New York and New England wine shops this Almaden is priced at around $1.50 a bottle—a great value for the money.

## CALIFORNIA PORT

Here the California wine makers are less successful than with sherry, and some of the big producers evidently don't care to try. They are interested in getting their port to market quickly and their objective is a highly flavoured drink that is sweet, potent, and cheap. One producer, Ficklin Vineyard, is generally regarded as the best in California.

## CENTRAL and SOUTHERN CALIFORNIA

As production records testify, over 200 million gallons of wine is produced yearly in California and, since the table wines of the north coast counties account for less than a third of this total, what fills the gap? Vast quantities of high-potency 'dessert' wines are made (manufactured would be a more appropriate word) in the central valley and further south, a region too hot for fine table wine grapes. Much of the product is shipped to other parts of the country in tank cars and bottled locally in gallon and half-gallon jugs. These are fortified wines, produced from various high-yield grape varieties and from culls, etc. With respect to sherry, this agglomeration is called *Shermat* (sherry material) by the wine makers. These wines are designated as port, sherry, muscatel, *et al.* Their chief attribute is their low-cost kick potential. They certainly are no kin to the sound, healthful, natural wines of the north coast counties and are small credit (except in balance sheets) to the U.S. wine industry.

## NEW YORK STATE WINES

Though wine is grown in many States, the only area of importance, after California, is in New York State in a small district known as Finger Lakes. This is lovely country and well worth a visit. The vineyards climb the steep hills that rise from the shores of the lake and the deep water mitigates for them the severity of the hard winter. Here some excellent dry, white, table wines are produced largely from vines native to the eastern sea-board. Summers in this section, near the northern limit of the wine belt, are too short and the climate too severe for the successful cultivation of the European species, the *Vitis vinifera* grown in California.[1]

Wine making began here around 1850 and the wines of those years must have had a harsh 'foxy' flavour, but these wild vines have been tamed and developed in the past thirty years or so and a few varieties now yield most agreeable wines. They are unlike any other wines in the world and surely this is the best reason in the world why they never should have been paraded under French and German names. Happily, however, the better table wines of the district now are turning more

[1] Dr Konstantin Frank, a European-trained viticulturist, has succeeded in producing really fine vinifera wines from vines growing on native root stocks. just as they do in France. A delightful one of these is his *Johannisberg Riesling Spätlese*.

and more to varietal names and it is these that you should get to know: *Delaware, Diamond, Diana, Elvira* and *Salem*—all white grapes. There are also local trade names such as Keuka Rosé (Keuka being one of the lakes) and Lake Country Red.

A change of much significance for the future is now taking place in the production of light table wines. This is the increasing use of French-American hybrids which yield wines unlike any hitherto produced in the region. In the decade following 1870 most French vineyards were laid waste by an American root louse called Phylloxera which had found its way to France and nearly every vine had to be replaced by grafting the age-old vinifera varieties on to Phylloxera-resistant American roots. This was an enormous task and ways were sought to avoid continuing it indefinitely. One solution appeared to be in the development of hybrid types which would combine the highly desirable[1] properties of the *Vitis vinifera* with resistance to the devastating pest.

There are many vineyard owners but few make their grapes into wine. This is done by four large companies which dominate the industry and normally contract in advance for the grapes. Much of the total output of these wineries is made up of different grape varieties,

[1] Though these hybrids have been successfully cultivated and are widely grown, it is a fact that most of the great wines of France are made from the traditional *Vitis vinifera* grafted to American root stocks. No hybrid has so far yielded the truly great red and white wines of France.

These hybrids offered a challenge to American viticulturists of the eastern States and in recent years a number of them, imported from France, have been successfully bred to withstand the severe winters of the Finger Lakes district. Many, in fact, are not only able to do this with little or no winter protection but are actually outproducing the true native varieties.

occasionally supplemented by low-cost wine from California. These blends go to market as 'Chablis', 'Claret', 'Burgundy', 'Sauterne' [*sic*] or Rhine (wine) though they have scant resemblance to these European wines. No wine lover could enlarge on the fine attributes of a New York State 'Burgundy'. Vast quantities of 'Port' and 'Sherry' are also made.

But New York State has another feather in its cap— Champagne. There are two leading producers: Pleasant Valley Wine Company, maker of *Great Western*, and Gold Seal Vineyards, maker of *Charles Fournier Brut*. Monsieur Fournier, a Frenchman who was at one time associated with Veuve Cliquot in France, is President of Gold Seal.

# Sherry and Port

Sherry is made in Spain, Port in Portugal. Both are fortified wines as distinguished from natural wines, which are the result of the simple fermentation of the juice of wine grapes. Both sherry and port start life as natural wines but in their production grape spirit (brandy) is added, and this raises the alcohol to around 20 per cent.

Vast quantities of so-called sherries and ports are made in other countries where wine is grown. In appearance and taste some of them resemble the genuine article—and they cost less. But if you are not already acquainted with these great wines from Spain and Portugal I hope you will become familiar with them before you accustom your palate to the imitations. A few of these are excellent, but it is idle to pretend that any matches the best of the originals.

Neither sherry nor port is a beverage wine to be drunk throughout a meal. Sherry is an ideal aperitif, especially if the meal to follow will include a fine wine. A couple of martinis or highballs will hamper a full appreciation of the wine. Moreover, though rather high in alcohol, sherry is a wine, not a spirit, and naturally goes better with wine. A glass of good sherry instead of a cocktail may surprise and delight your guests. It will have at least the merit of novelty.

Apart from its role as an aperitif, sherry is the ideal wine of hospitality to the casual caller. Last winter I called one day on my old friend André Simon at about 11 o'clock in the morning. As is his custom, he offered me a glass of sherry—a dry Fino. What other drink could be appropriate at that hour?

A sweeter sherry—an Oloroso, for example—served with shortbread cookies or other dry cakes, makes a delightful change from tea in the afternoon. And it has the advantage of being always ready—no water to boil, no teapot—instant hospitality. And as good cooks know, sherry is a useful ingredient in the preparation of many dishes. But use a good sherry (or Madeira) for this. The so-called 'cooking' sherry is likely to do more harm than good.

While sherry is for the late forenoon, the afternoon at tea time, and as an aperitif replacing cocktails, port is primarily an after-dinner drink. In many English homes it has been a 'must' for 150 years. A quaint ritual which still persists is one you may like to indulge in when you entertain your English friends at a dinner party. It goes like this: the meal is finished. The ladies withdraw to the *with*drawing-room where, with no men around, they relax and enjoy their feminine conversation. Their departure leaves more room around the table and the men reseat themselves in comfort, pushing their chairs at an angle and crossing their legs.

It is the moment for port. They are alone; not even the butler (if there were one) dare enter the dining room unless summoned. The host does not serve his guests individually. The bottle or decanter of port is passed round the table clockwise, starting with the man at the host's left. As it is passed from man to man each guest fills his glass and the decanter thus returns to the host who now serves himself. There it rests until someone accepts his invitation to have another glass. No matter where that person is sitting the decanter is again passed round the table from man to man—never across the table. When the men have had enough port, or when conversation lags, the host proposes 'Shall we join the ladies?' It is an interesting conceit.

The lighter ports are appropriate also as an aperitif preceding lunch.

The wine which is to become sherry is grown in the south-western corner of Spain. All the genuine sherry in the world comes from some 24,000 acres of chalky soil, planted for the most part to the Palomino grape. The special character of the wine is due to an unusual combination of soils and climate that exists nowhere else. A number of vineyards in California are planted to the Palomino and the wines they yield are made into California sherry. Though the vines were brought from Spain, the soil and climate cannot be imported and the best end product can never be quite like the fine sherries from Spain. I am glad to say, however, that some very good 'sherry' is made in California.

The making of sherry is a complicated process. Following its normal fermentation, brandy is added—from one to five gallons per hundred gallons of wine. The wine is then run off into casks which are not filled full and which are left in the open with the bungs loose to admit the surrounding air. There they lie in all weathers, in the heat and the cold, some under roof and others not, and after a time the wine begins a sort of second fermentation. This, with the lighter types of wine, is induced by the growth on the surface of the wine of a yeast called *flor*—Spanish for flower. This period lasts for about eighteen months. The wine is then

A typical solera in a Spanish bodega. Note replenishment of casks in top row. *Photo courtesy of Harveys of Bristol.*

drawn off clear and bright and begins its protracted stay in the *bodegas*—storage warehouses. Here these wines constitute what is called a *criadera*, or nursery, where they 'grow up' under careful observation. Eventually they will be incorporated in a solera.

This consists of rows of casks placed on top of one another, usually four tiers high. The solera is old—often a hundred years or more—and the oldest wine is in the bottom row. The necessary ageing of sherry takes place in the solera, and it is from the solera that wine is drawn for the final blending and bottling. The blender starts with a quantity of wine from the top row of casks, a smaller quantity from the third row, less from the second row and finally a very small quantity from the bottom row. The solera is replenished by wine from the row immediately above and with wine from a criadera in the top row.

The types offered by most shippers are: *Fino*, the driest of all, *Amontillado*, less dry and rather more delicate, *Oloroso*, medium sweet, and *Cream* (or Golden Brown), heavy, sweet and dark in colour. Shippers give their own brand names to these four types and the wine will vary according to the shippers' ideas and the demands of their clientele. The label reproduced on the following page describes the sherry Monsieur Simon invited me to drink. You would order it by asking for *La Riva's Tres Palmas*. It is a very dry Fino.

The important point to remember about sherry is that it does not improve in bottle. There's no point in including sherry in your wine cellar—except, of course, as a matter of convenience.

Port is made from grapes grown in northern Portugal, in the valley of the Douro river which meets the sea at Oporto. Port, the wine, gets its name from Oporto, the seaport. It is made from grapes of many varieties, grown in hundreds of vineyards. The wine that is to become port is made in the valley and stored there until the following spring when it is floated down the Douro in flat-bottomed boats to shippers' lodges across the river from Oporto. It is now the property of the shippers, most of them English firms and some of them well on 200 years of age. Port is the result of the skill of these famous English shippers who, in the first half of the eighteenth century, learned how to convert these quite ordinary wines into a beverage which dominated the English wine trade for seven generations.

On its arrival at the shippers' lodges, experts test, taste and classify the wines. If the vintage has been good, the best of this wine will be set aside to become *Vintage*

*Port.* It must be good, for vintage port is the wine of one year only and imperfections cannot be corrected by blending with other wines. It is left 'in the wood', i.e. in long thin barrels called 'pipes', for eighteen months to two years and is then shipped (probably 90 per cent of it) to England where it is bottled. Once in bottle it is put away to mature in the shippers' cellars or is sold to persons who can afford to buy today the wine that their children and grandchildren will drink. The big shippers hold large stocks and they are of great value.

The rest of the new wine which came down the river from the vineyards will form blending stocks and become in the end either *Tawny Port* or *Ruby Port*. It will be classified with these two kinds in mind—the better wines being earmarked for Tawny, the remainder for Ruby.

The wines are blended in huge vats, some of them holding as much as 10,000 gallons. When the desired blend is achieved, the wine is run off into pipes, there to shed some of its fire. At this point the wine will be dark red—often almost purple—and hardly drinkable.

In the wood it will lose its harshness and some of its colour. The longer it remains in cask the lighter the colour will become. So it is obvious that *the lighter the colour* of Tawny, *the older it will be* and the smoother. Beware, though, that your 'Pale Old Tawny' comes from a highly reputable shipper. If not, you may get a relatively young wine that has had its deep red colour made 'tawny' by the addition of white port—or by some other means. Genuine Tawny cannot be but old; it is the finest port obtainable except very old vintage port.

Ruby is a blend of younger wines and less care has been spent on it by the blender. Obviously it will be the cheapest of the three, since it can be, and is, marketed when quite young. Both Tawny and Ruby are left in the wood to mature and are bottled by the shipper as required to meet his customers' demands.

Port is a wine which suffers, perhaps more than any other, at the hands of unscrupulous wine manipulators. A very large percentage of the 'port' offered in the low to medium class markets anywhere in the world is a concocted liquid masquerading under an honourable name to which it has no right. It may not be far from the truth to say that the bulk of the American product falls in this category. *Good port cannot be low in price.*

# Madeira and Marsala

Like sherry and port, these are fortified wines. Madeira comes from the Portuguese island of Madeira, in the Atlantic 400 miles off the coast of north-west Africa. It has a temperate, almost semi-tropical, climate. The wine is much like sherry as to its use—an ideal aperitif and the perfect wine of hospitality. If you habitually offer sherry to your friends and guests, give them a surprise by proposing Madeira. It may be new to some of them, and it has an interesting history.

Wine has been made in Madeira for more than 500 years but the wine we know today dates from America's later colonial period and the first decades of our independence. It was one of the favourites of Washington, Jefferson, Madison and Franklin, and the wealthy planters of the South always had ample stocks on hand. It was something of a 'status symbol'—a 'must' in patrician circles.

Madeira came to the colonies and became popular due largely to a provision in English law at the time, which required all European wines imported by the colonists to be carried in English bottoms, i.e. shipped first to England (and taxed) and then to Boston, Philadelphia and Charleston. But for some reason, whether by design or oversight, Madeira was exempt from this requirement. Consequently Madeira was cheap compared with other European wines. Julian Street, in his book, *Wines*,[1] tells of a 'Boston Wine-

[1] Alfred Knopf, 1933. Revised edition.

Party' which occurred five years before the famed 'Boston Tea-Party'. The sloop *Liberty* smuggled into Boston Harbour a cargo of Madeira, but was seized there by the British warship *Romney*. Ship and shipment belonged, however, to one John Hancock who was not slow in rousing the town, and along the waterfront bottles flew when the townsfolk rescued the wine.

Madeira is made like any other natural wine and when fermentation is complete brandy is added to bring the alcohol up to 18–20 per cent. It is then run off into casks, called 'pipes', and placed in heated warehouses— *estufas*. Here it is held at controlled temperatures for periods which may vary from 3 to 6 months. Madeira is not a wine that wants to be kept in a cool cellar and it is preferable to stand bottles upright rather than place them horizontally in the usual wine bins. From the estufas the wine is transferred to appropriate soleras similar to those used in the ageing and blending of sherry.

There are three principal types of Madeira: *Sercial*, which is dry, *Bual* (or Boal), which is sweet, and *Malmsey*, sweeter still. There is also one called *Verdelho* which is much like Sercial but not widely distributed in this country. All of these names are those of grape varieties. On my birthday in December 1965 André Simon[1] came to us for lunch and brought me, as a birthday present, a bottle of Sercial of the 1864 vintage. The date can be accepted as accurate for the bottle was given to

[1] Monsieur Simon, now in his ninetieth year, was for many years in the Champagne trade in England. During those days and since, he has written almost continuously on wine and food and the art of good living and has some fifty books to his credit. In 1933 he founded the Wine and Food Society and has been its President ever since.

Monsieur Simon with pride when, earlier in the year, he visited the island on his way back from South Africa where he had spent the winter. I felt flattered that my old friend had chosen to give it to me. As I was about to open it he stopped me by saying; 'Oh, not now; you must keep it for your old age.'

One of the good things about Madeira is that it is not imitated as sherry is. So far as I know there is no such thing as California Madeira, or New York State Madeira, or South African or Australian. If the label says Madeira, the wine in the bottle was made on the Island. So we are spared the cheap imitations. There are so many spurious sherries on the market that when offered 'A glass of sherry?' one *feels* like asking 'What *kind* of sherry?' You run no such risk with Madeira. This is not to say, though, that all Madeiras are good; it depends, as with nearly all wines, on the wine maker, or blender, and the shipper. There are many fine Houses—most of them in England.

Madeira is used extensively by the top chefs of the world in cooking. By most of them it is considered preferable to sherry.

MARSALA

Marsala is a fortified wine from Sicily. It closely re-sembles sherry from Spain. Normally a dry wine, it is made sweet by the addition of very sweet concentrated grape juice. In contrast with most Italian wines, pro-duction of Marsala is under strict Government control as to alcohol and degree of sweetness. Marsala is an aperitif wine but it is also widely used in Italian cooking.

# Fermentation

The juice of all wine grapes when ripe consists chiefly of sugar and water. In the process of fermentation this grape sugar undergoes a chemical transformation by which it is broken down into nearly equal parts of alcohol and carbon dioxide gas. It is this gas which makes the must bubble and get warm as fermenting proceeds. Fermentation is induced by microscopic yeast cells which, floating in the air, attach themselves to the ripening grapes, forming a visible 'bloom' on the skins. In some cases, particularly in northern wine growing regions—in New York State and in Germany—if the grapes are a bit unripe when finally they must be harvested, sugar is added to the must to ensure proper fermentation.

When the grapes are crushed these living micro-organisms enter the juice and bring about this simple chemical transformation. The gas passes off in bubbles and the alcohol remains in the pure water which was the major constituent of the juice. This is wine. If fermentation is complete, i.e. if all the sugar is thus transformed, it is a very dry wine. If some of the sugar remains it is a sweet wine.

An interesting point about fermentation is that no matter how much sugar the grapes contain the alcohol content of the wine will not rise much above 14 or 15 per cent. When that degree of alcohol is reached, fermentation will stop because the alcohol kills the yeast. Most of the grapes grown in the Sauternais in

France contain this excess of sugar. That is why these wines are often so sweet.

In a preceding chapter, 'What is Wine?', it is said that the grapes are *promptly* crushed after being gathered from the vines. If they are not the 'bloom' will be lost and fermentation will be faulty.

In some areas unsuitable for the growth of wine grapes—in England, for example, and in this country far from any vineyard—city 'wineries' make wine from dehydrated, crushed grapes. The dried grapes arrive in bags or other containers and are dumped into huge vats where water and yeast are added. Kept at a moderate temperature this reconstructed must will ferment and something like wine will result. No wine produced by this method can be as good or as wholesome as the natural product made at the vineyard winery. This wine has the colour and alcoholic strength of the natural product but it is no credit to the wine industry.

# Wine Vintages

Wines grown in Europe vary in their nature and quality from year to year and from district to district. This variation is chiefly due to the weather which may be favourable in one year and unfavourable in the next—good in one section while poor in another. A poor year in Germany may be a good year in France—a poor year in Bordeaux may be a good year in Burgundy. It is rare that any year is poor everywhere.

This is why vintage charts that list good and poor years without regard to *where* are sure to be misleading. If you are buying fine wines to stock your cellar you will need a comprehensive report on vintages[1] covering at least the past ten years plus the guidance of a competent wine merchant. But for those with whom wine is a daily habit the matter of vintage can be simplified as follows:

In the decade 1954–1963 there were *three poor years* in most of France and Germany—*1954, 1956 and 1960*. In five of those ten years most of the wines were rated 'good', and in two—*1959 and 1961*—they were classed as 'great' or 'very great'. I am sure that this is already too much to remember; so forget it. The years to remember, and so *avoid* them, are the three poor years—1954, 1956, and 1960. Get these engraved on your memory, particularly 1960—a bad year very nearly everywhere. Any of the other seven will be all right and you might keep 1959 and 1961 in mind as specially

[1] The best ones I have seen are those prepared by Frank Schoonmaker and in recent years published in *Gourmet* magazine, and sometimes reprinted in small booklet form.

worth buying either to lay away, or for some special occasion tomorrow or next week.

As to American wines there is not much need to be concerned with their vintage; in fact it is somewhat rare to find it stated on labels. There are two good reasons for this. The good table wines of California are grown in the area near San Francisco Bay and here there is little variation in the weather from year to year. This is not true to the same extent in the Finger Lakes district of New York State. Late spring frost or too much rain in August and September will make a lot of difference. The second reason, applicable to both regions, with respect to the less costly table wines, is that many of these wines are standard blends which will be made up of wines of two or more years. This is common practice and is not in any way objectionable. All non-vintage French Champagnes are blends, and so are many of the regional wines of France and Germany.

And remember that while age is desirable in many great and good wines, youth is a virtue in a number of others. These, as you have already learned, are at their best when quite young. For this reason vintage is often not stated on labels. But if it is it works in reverse; it enables you to avoid buying a wine that is *too old to be good*. Look with suspicion on a Beaujolais or a Tavel that is more than five or six years old. It must have got side-tracked somewhere along the line on its journey from the vineyard to you. Many of the white wines of Germany and those of Alsace and the Loire in France are best drunk when quite young.

# Appellation Contrôlée

In 1964 this country imported over three million gallons of wine grown and bottled in France. Of this quantity, 90 per cent—13 million bottles—bore on their labels the words *Appellation Contrôlée*. The words are full of significance. Frank Schoonmaker, in his excellent *Encyclopedia of Wine*,[1] says of them: 'They are the consumer's principal protection and his best friend, and of enormous value to all honest (wine) producers as well.'

In preceding chapters I have emphasized the importance of reliance on the character and reputation of the shippers and importers when choosing your wines. This is sound advice but it is not always easy to know the reputation and character of the gentlemen of the wine trade and when you don't know you can rely, with respect to French wines, on *Appellation Contrôlée*. In fact if these words are on the label you can relax your vigilance as to the shipper and the importer.

Appellation Contrôlée is short for Appellation d'Origine Contrôlée (AOC) (controlled designation of origin). The name of a wine, as you have learned, is the name of the place where the grapes were grown and the name you use when buying your wines. If you ask for a bottle of *Beaujolais Supérieur*, the AOC, backed by the power of three departments of the French Government —Agriculture, Finance and Justice—guarantees that the wine in the bottle was produced in strict accord

[1] Hastings House, 1964, 410 pp. $6.95.

with the stipulated regulations applicable to the vineyard areas in Beaujolais entitled to label their wine
*Beaujolais Supérieur, Appellation Contrôlée*. You will see
what these regulations are like if you refer to the des-
cription of Beaujolais on page 49, and again in the para-
graphs on Chablis on page 51.

AOC was created in 1935 by an Order in Council of
the French Government. This Order called for the
setting up of a NATIONAL COMMITTEE OF APPELLATIONS
OF ORIGIN OF WINES AND BRANDIES. Its first task was to
review the boundaries of the districts in which better
than ordinary wines were grown. The wine of these
districts had long been called by the traditional district
name but the boundaries of districts were, in most cases,
not rigidly fixed. Nothing prevented a wine grower in
Beaujolais or Chablis—or anywhere else—from stretching the yield of his vineyard by adding to his own wine,
wine grown somewhere else. At one time many of the
wine growers of Châteauneuf-du-Pape were threatened
almost with extinction by cheap wine brought in from
other areas and sold as Chateauneuf-du-Pape. The
reader will recall that this practice seriously hurt the
honest producers in both Beaujolais and Chablis—and,
of course in many other wine districts. AOC effectively
prevents such chicanery by *stipulating the maximum yield* of
wine that can be made within the boundary of a given
'appellation'.

It is simple enough for the authorities to enforce
observance of these limitations. Every grower in the
fixed area must record each year the quantity of wine
made and of deliveries from the declared volume to
négociants and consumers. Moreover, each withdrawal

of wine from his cellars must be accompanied by a Green Circulation voucher on which a transfer, or movement, tax of Fr. 5.80 ($1.15) per hectolitre must be paid. All of these documents are open to scrutiny by officers of the AOC. And you may be sure that the wary eyes of neighbouring vineyardists are quick to spot any infraction of the rules. The penalties for such fraud are severe—heavy fines and in extreme cases imprisonment.

Today the wines of 246 areas are entitled to a 'controlled appellation'. Of the total wine production of France in 1964 only about 15 per cent was grown in AOC-controlled areas. Fortunately for American wine lovers, most of the French wine imported into this country is in the 'Appellation Contrôlée' category.

There is, however, a secondary control system, also administered by AOC. This was designed some years ago to do justice to those producers whose wine, though honestly made and marketed, could not fully measure up to the high standards of AOC. This category was created to bridge the gap between the vast volume of *vin ordinaire* and wines deserving of something better. These wines are called *Vins Délimités de Qualité Supérieure*, VDQS—Wines of Superior Quality from Delimited Areas. These growers produce much good, sound wine which is honestly made, and it should cost a bit less in wineshops than *district wines* with AOC controlled appellations. They are identified on labels by the monogram stamp. Try them.

# Starting a Wine Cellar

That you have bought and are reading this guide means that you are interested in wine and want to know more about it. I hope you will make wine with your meals a daily habit. It can do you nothing but good. But whether you have wine every day or serve it only occasionally, the collection of a few dozen bottles, carefully chosen, is a most engaging hobby.

In earlier times a wine cellar was a cool, dark room in the cellar of a big house with wine bins all round the walls, stocked with wines many of which had been 'laid down' by a preceding generation of wine lovers. The door to this cellar was under lock and key—a key which the owner of the house jealously guarded. This kind of wine cellar is fast becoming extinct. But the romantic name remains and now designates simply a store of wines kept in the house or apartment. The photo on page 127 is of my 'cellar' in our apartment in London. Originally a coat closet, it is off the entrance hall and will be cool both in winter and summer.

One of the fascinating things about having a wine cellar is the stocking of it at the start and the replacement of bottles as they are consumed. Take your time doing this. If you have in mind a few wines that you know and like, start with these and then buy one bottle at a time of others that you fancy. Of those that fulfil your expectations, buy two or three for the cellar. When dining with friends, if the wine served pleases you, ask your host the name of it and of the importer, or of the shop where he bought it. You could not pay him a more pleasing compliment. Then buy two or three bottles for your own cellar. Further on I tell you what my cellar contains today but it would be a mistake to go out and order the wines mentioned, though you could try some of them and see how you like them. Some of the advice given in the chapter 'How Can I Tell?' will be useful here.

If in your household wine is a daily habit you doubtless have some favourites among the less costly wines. Get at least a dozen bottles of these. It's convenient to have them on hand, and wine is cheaper by the case. Also you rid yourself of the chore of buying wine every week along with the groceries.

During our stay of some months in London our daily wine was usually a Claret or Burgundy type from the Rioja (ree-o-ha) district in Spain. The wine was clear and sound and cost about $1.20 a bottle. For a change to something a bit better we bought good district wines from Bordeaux and Burgundy—Margaux, Saint Emilion, Beaujolais Village, Nuits-St-Georges, Pommard. Recently in Connecticut our daily wine was either one of the less costly red wines of California or a Rioja which, though imported in bottle from Spain, was sold at retail for $1.25 a bottle—a good value.

As to the mechanics of setting up a wine cellar, if you live in a house and your basement is reasonably dry you will probably find space in it suitable for a wine cellar, but few today can provide this ideal accommodation. The alternative is a closet or cupboard situated away from any source of heat and one which can be reasonably well ventilated. Your chief problem will be to find

Photo of my 'cellar' in our London flat.

this storage space where the air is *cool enough in winter*. Summer heat will not bother you if the closet is in a shaded area, presumably in the northern part of the dwelling. If the temperature can be held within the limits of 15 degrees above or below 55 degrees Fahrenheit your fine wines will keep in good condition.

When you have found the space, make or buy racks or bins to hold the number of bottles you are likely to have in your cellar—perhaps four dozen. Wire or wood-

and-metal bins, each holding a dozen bottles, are readily obtainable. Or your wine merchant will give you discarded wooden whisky cases. Arrange the bins so they will be more or less at eye level and with the compartments readily accessible on opening the door. Place the bottles in the bins with the necks facing outwards. It will be useful to label the bins holding fine old wines so you can withdraw a wanted bottle without disturbing others.

When you begin stocking your cellar a point to be emphasized, first and foremost, is that *dry* wines should predominate.

The reason for this is that sweet wines are wholly unsuitable to be drunk in any quantity with your food.

As to my own cellar (in London where I normally spend a few months each year), I have just taken an inventory. This is what it contains today—April 1965:

Two bottles of non-Vintage Champagne:
  Pommery Greno
  Mumm's Cordon Rouge
Four bottles of red Bordeaux:
  Château Kirwan 1955
  Château Ausone 1960
  Château Talbot 1959
  Château Gruaud Larose 1955
Two bottles of white Graves:
  Château Olivier 1959
  Château Carbonnieux 1961
Six bottles of red Burgundy:
  Four Bonnes-Mares 1955
  One Pommard 1961
  One Nuits-St Georges 1959
Two bottles of Beaujolais:
  Fleurie 1961
  Morgon 1961
Three bottles of white Burgundy:
  Two Meursault 1959
  One Montrachet 1955

One bottle of Sauternes:
  Château Filhot 1955
Three bottles of Rhône (red):
  Côte Rotie 1961
  Chante Alouette 1959
  Hermitage 1955
Two bottles of Moselle:
  Berncastler Doctor 1961
  Gracher Domprobst 1962
Two bottles of Rhine wine:
  Niersteiner Rehbach 1963
  Zeltinger Himmelreich 1963
Two bottles Madeira:
  One Sercial
  One Bual
One bottle sherry:
  La Riva's Fino
Three bottles of Spanish 'Claret'.

Thirty-three bottles costing about $75. If this 'cellar' were in our Connecticut house it would contain perhaps a dozen bottles of American wines.


# On Ordering Wine in a Restaurant[1]


Though the point is often over-emphasized, it is true that wines and foods have their affinities. Some are more appropriate than others to accompany certain foods. So it is necessary to decide on the food before you order the wine you will drink with it. Having composed your menu to the satisfaction of your companion and

[1] An informal three-course meal with friends.

guests, ask for the Wine List, called in French restaurants the *Carte des Vins*.

The waiter who has just taken your order, instead of bringing the wine list to you, may beckon the wine waiter, *sommelier*, in French, and this may precipitate a minor problem. He can be helpful or he can be a nuisance. Most wine waiters in any but first-class restaurants and hotels know precious little about wines, but they are quite ready to give you advice, based presumably on what other customers are ordering or on stocks in the cellar that are not moving fast enough. Obviously their recommendations are worthless.

It is not difficult to spot this type of wine waiter and it is easy to get rid of him. Just look up from the wine list and politely say: 'We'd like to think about this for a bit; would you come back in a few moments.' This gets him away from your elbow and also lets him know that you have ideas of your own on what wines to order. Now you can take time to study the list and discuss it with your friends. You may be sure that if you have read and absorbed the facts in this guide you know a good deal more about wines than he does. Select your wines and when the wine waiter returns to your table, give him the order confidently and without discussion.

On the other hand the competent wine waiter can be most helpful. You will not want him to tell you what *types* of wine to choose (you already know that) but in making your selections he will be able to answer any specific questions on the wines listed. Usually the wine list will give no more than the name of the wine and its vintage. As has previously been stated, your best guide to quality and authenticity of a given wine will be the names of the shipper and of the importer. If he doesn't know them he will, if you ask him, fetch the bottle so that you may study the label. As soon as he sees that you know something about wines, and know what you want, he will, if he is qualified for his job, become interested. If he is co-operative and attentive to the service you will rightly feel that he is entitled to a good share of the tip when you pay your check.

At the end of the meal, when you are doing this and have calculated the amount of the tip, divide it between the waiter and the wine waiter, roughly in the proportion of the relative cost of the food and the wine. Give the waiter his share and if the wine waiter isn't at hand, ask the waiter to send him to you. It would be asking too much should you give the full amount to the waiter and ask him to 'take care of' the wine waiter. Moreover, you should *see* the wine waiter and thus show your appreciation of his good service.

Now to get back to the beginning—what wines to order with the food. The basic fact to keep in mind is that *red wine rebels at fish* and all sea food. If you start with oysters, lobsters, crab or any kind of fish, only a dry white wine will be appropriate. 'Chablis with oysters' is a well-founded dictum but if a good French Chablis is not available (there are hundreds of imitations) any other good, dry wine will do just as well—a white Burgundy, a Moselle or a Rhine wine.

For the meat course, I and most others, I think, prefer red wine with beef or game. The almost universally accepted 'rule'—'red meat, red wine'—owes its origin, in a negative sense, to the undeniable fact that red wine does *not* go with fish.

You will have ordered white wine with the fish; now choose a good red wine for the meat. The choice is virtually unlimited. Another advantage of red wine is that if any of it is left at the end of the meat course it will be most appropriate with the cheese which may follow. If you are more than four at a table you will need more than one bottle of the red wine and, again, interest will be added if the second bottle is not a repeat of the first. When considering the wines you can decide on this but don't order it along with the first. When the first bottle is empty, call the wine waiter and order the second.

Now you come to the sweet or dessert, and if there are no more than four at table a half bottle will be enough. A good Sauternes will suit best, and the order should be given to the wine waiter at the beginning so that he can provide the necessary small glasses and also see that the wine is chilled. If you are having both sweets and cheese the cheese should precede the sweet.

Presumably coffee will follow and if you wish to serve a liqueur with it Cognac is to be preferred. Here you will offer your guests a choice and some of them may prefer a sweet liqueur—for example a Grand Marnier, Benedictine, or our own American Southern Comfort— an excellent liqueur. All that remains is relaxation and bright conversation.

But this whole matter can be disposed of at one stroke by drinking champagne from start to finish.

NOTE: If you want fully to enjoy these wines with your meal you should not have cocktails (gin or whisky) beforehand. Have instead a glass of sherry, dry or medium dry, a dry Madeira or a wine-based aperitif such as Dubonnet, Campari or a plain vermouth. Or, better still, Champagne.

# On Serving Wines at Home[1]

What has been said in a preceding chapter on ordering wines at a restaurant applies, of course, to choosing wines for a lunch or dinner at home with friends. As you compose the menu you will decide also on the appropriate wines. If these are to come from your own cellar take the red wine from the bin the day before and place it in the dining room to lose its chill.

Red wines should always be served at room temperature. Never warm a cold bottle by artificial means such as standing it in a basin of warm water or on a radiator. The taste of wine and its aroma will be improved if the cork is withdrawn an hour or two before the wine is to be served. White wine should be chilled—but not too cold; icing it will rob it of its flavour. If the wines are not from your own stock, buy them if you can, a few days beforehand so that they may rest quietly. This is specially important with fine old wines.

Glasses should be provided for each of the wines if there are more than one. In this case there are three: place them in a group to the right of the place plate. Plain, uncoloured, rather large glasses are best. Green-tinted glasses for German or Alsatian wines are to be found in many glassware departments. Let them remain there. Any colour in the glass will rob the wine of its own lovely colour. Glasses need not be expensive; acceptable ones of good design can be had at Wool-

[1] Assuming six intimate friends at table with one or no maid to help serve. The dinner consists of three courses: shrimp cocktail, roast rib of beef, almond cake with fruit salad and ice cream.

Monsieur André Simon at lunch with us in our London apartment.

worths for 40 cents, much better ones in department stores at $1.50 and Baccarat from France at Tiffany's at $6. The same style and size of glass should be used for both red and white still wines but champagne calls for its own glass.

Wine is poured by the host while the food is being served. He stands up and walks around the table pouring the wine into each glass without regard to 'ladies first'. No glass should be filled more than half full. The host will pour a small amount first into his own glass. This gesture arises from the fact that a bit of cork might emerge and if so it will be in his own glass and he can remove it. In a restaurant the wine waiter will pour a bit of wine into the host's glass so that he may taste and approve or reject it. Taste it and don't hesitate to reject it if it is faulty.

134

When the first course is finished and the second is being served, the host again serves each person. During the meal he will keep an eye on everyone's glass and replenish it when it is nearly empty.

If a wine is served with the sweet (unless it be champagne) it is preferable to serve it from a small carafe. Here a fine piece of cut glass adds its charm. If a liqueur is served with the coffee the host will again 'do the honours' either at table or in the drawing room.

If champagne is the wine served with the meal the host should withdraw the cork at the table, and this takes a bit of practice to avoid a popping cork and probably loss of wine with sometimes rather embarrassing consequences.

WINE GLASSES

In much of the commercial literature on wine—the leaflet you pick up in a wine shop—far too much is often made of the matter of wine glasses. Designs are shown of a glass for Bordeaux, another for Burgundy, another for Rhine and Moselle wines, one for Alsatian and one for Anjou and Vouvray. This, of course, borders on the absurd.

The simple truth is that wine looks best and tastes best when drunk from plain, crystal clear stem glasses. Cut glass, lovely for water, is inappropriate for wine.

By plain I mean a simple, round shape, slightly incurving at the top and neither coloured, etched nor engraved. It makes no difference whether for Bordeaux or Burgundy or for red or white wine. As to size, a glass appropriate for still wines will hold 8 or 9 ounces. When your menu calls for both red and white wine it is preferable to use a slightly smaller glass (of the same pattern) for the white wine. Remember that a wine glass should never be filled more than half full.

For sweet wines, served with desserts, the glass should be smaller—4 or 5 ounces—and the sides preferably straight. For champagne the correct glass is of tulip shape—never the saucer type, popular fifty years ago.

For sherry, port, madeira, etc., a smaller tulip shape is suitable but a rather more attractive glass will have a deep bowl, very slightly incurved and with a shorter stem.

With the finer wines the cork will be branded as shown above. This is a positive guide that the wine is authentic. When you order a costly wine in a restaurant the wine waiter should hand you the cork for inspection. If he doesn't; ask him for it.

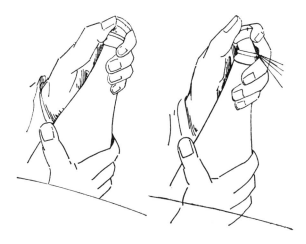

This is how to open a bottle of champagne. It is best to stand up for this. Untwist the wire and remove it and the gilt foil from the cork. Take care that the cork doesn't shoot out and hit the ceiling. The cork should be tight in the bottle-neck even after the wire is removed. But sometimes it isn't; so be careful. If it is loose hold it if you can while the gas escapes around it. If it is tight pry it free, pushing with the thumbs, and then, twisting—not the cork but the bottle—bring the cork almost out. Now tip it very slightly to one side to allow the gas to escape silently. If this is done with care there will be no 'pop' or loss of wine. As a precaution the host should have his own glass handy in case the wine bubbles over.

Of course, if you *want* the excitement of the popping cork, just loosen it with the thumbs and then aim the bottle at whatever target you wish. —but above the heads of your guests. A flying cork can cause a really serious injury.

# Pronunciation Guide

Words preceded by the article *Le*, *La*, or *Les* are placed under L or under the initial letter of the noun, e.g. Les Grands Echezeaux is indexed under G while Les Loges and Les Preuses are to be found under L.

Amigny: am-meen-yee
Ausone (Ch.): oh-zone
d'Arche: darsh

Baumes: bome
Beaune: bone
Beauregard (Ch.): bo-ray-gar
Beychevelle (Ch.): bash-uh-vell
Blanchots: blawn-sho
Bonnezeaux: bonne-ay-zo
Bougros: boo-gro
Bouscaut (Ch.): boos-ko
Brouilly: broo-yee
Bué: bew-ay

Caillou (Ch.): ky-yoo
Calon-Ségur (Ch.): cal-awn-say-goor
Cantemerle (Ch.): cawn-tuh-mairl
Carbonnieux (Ch.): car-bawn-yuh
cave or caves: caav
Certan (Ch.): sair-tawn
Chablis: shab-lee
Chaintré: shan-tray
Chambertin: shawm-bair-tan
Chantalouettes: schan-tal-you-ette
Charmes: sharm
Chassagne: shass-anya
Châteauneuf du Pape: sha-toe-nuff-due-pap
Chauvin (Ch.): sho-van
Chavignol (Ch.): sha-veen-yol
Chénas: shay-nass
Chiroubles: sheer-roub'l
Climens: klee-mense
Clos de Bèze: klo-duh-bezz
Condrieu: cawn-dree-uh
Conséillante: cawn-say-yahnt

Corton: cor-tawn
Côte de Beaune: coat-duh-bone
Côte de Brouilly: coat-duh-broo-yee
Côte de Nuits: coat-duh-nwee
Côte Rotie: coat ro-tee
Couhins: koo-anse
Coutet: koo-tay
Croze-Hermitage: crows-air-mee-taj

l'Evangile (Ch.): lay-van-geel

Fargues: farg
Filhot (Ch.): fee-yo
Fines Roches (Ch.): feen-rawsh
La Fleur (Ch.): la flur
Fleurie: flur-ree

Gazin (Ch.): gaz-zan
Gevrey-Chambertin: jev-ray-shawm-bair-tan
Grand Corbin (Ch.): gran-cor-ban
Grand Mayne (Ch.): gran-main
Grands Echezeaux: Les, lay-grawn-zesh-shay-zo
Graves: graave, drop the 's'
Grenache: gren-ash
Grenouilles: gren-oo-yee
Grillet (Ch.): gree-yay
Guiraud (Ch.): ghee-ro

Haut-Brion (Ch.): oh-bree-awn
Haut Médoc: oh-may-dawk
Hermitage: air-mee-taj

Juliénas: jule-yea-nass

Lafite (Ch.): la feet
Lafite Rothschild (Ch.): la feet-rawt-sheeld

138

La Lagune (Ch.): la-lah-guhn
La Mothe (Ch.): la-mote
Laville Hâut-Brion (Ch.): la-veel-oh-bree-awn
Léoville-Poyferré (Ch.): lay-o-veal pawh-ferray
Le Clos: luh-klo
Les Clos: lay-klo
Le Mont Garcin (Ch.): le-mawn-gar-san
Les Loges: lay-lozjuh
Les Nues: lay-nieu
Les Preuses: lay preuz
Lochè: low shay
Lussac: lew-sack
Lynch-Bages: lansh baaj

Mâconnais: mac-con-nay
Margaux: mar-go
Médoc: may-dawk
Mission Haut-Brion, La (Ch.): mee-see-awn-oh-bree-awm
Meursault: mair-so
Mont Garcin, Le (Ch): mawn--gar-sawn
Montrose (Ch): mawn-rose
Morey-Saint-Denis: mo-ray-san-duh-nee
Morgon: maur-gawn
Moulin à Vent: moo-lahn-ah-vawn
Mouton Rothschild (Ch.): moo-tawn-rawt-sheeld
Musigny: moos-een-ye
Myrat (Ch.): mee-rah

Nénin (Ch.): nay-nan
Nozet (Ch.): no zay
Nuits-Saint-Georges: nwee-san-shorsh

Olivier (Ch.): oh-lee-vee-ay

Palmer (Ch.): pahl-mair
Pape Clement (Ch.): pap clay-mawn

Paradis, Le: pa-rah-dee
Pauillac: paw-yack
Petit, e.g. Petit Chablis: puh-tee-shab-lee
Petrus (Ch.): pet-trewss
Pierre Bontemps (Ch.): bonn-tawn
Pomerol: pawm-may-rawl
Pontet Canet (Ch.): pawn-teh-can-nay
Pouilly: poo-yee
Pouilly-Fuissé: poo-yee-fwee-say
Pouilly-Fumé: poo-yee-few-may
Puligny: poo-lean-ye
Preignac: prayn-yac
Premier Cru: prem-me-yea-crue
Puissegain (Ch.): pweece-gahn

Quarts de Chaume: car-duh-shome

Riesling: reece-ling
Rieussec: rhee-oo-sec
Romanée-Conti: ro-man-nay-cawn-tee

Sables: sab'l
Saint Amour: san-tam-mour
Saint Emilion: san-tay-meel-yon
Saint Estèphe: san-tess-steff
Saint Georges: san-shorj
Saint Julien: san-shoe-lee-an
Sancerre: san-sair
Saumur: so-muhr
Sauternes: so-tairne
Sauvignon: so-veen-yon
Solutre: so lou-tray
Suduiraut: sood-we-ro

Talbot (Ch.): tal-bo

Valmur: valmuire
Vaudesir: voo-day-zeer
Verdigny: vair-deen-yee
Vergisson: vair-ghee-sawn

# Index

141